THE MEANINGS OF MODERN ART

by JOHN RUSSELL

Art Critic, *The New York Times*

VOLUME **8**

A WORLD REMODELED

THE MUSEUM OF MODERN ART, NEW YORK

I. Marc Chagall
Forward! 1917
Art Gallery of Ontario, Toronto

It is one of the most resilient of human illusions that some day, somewhere, we shall be granted a fresh start in life.

To what else, after all, do we owe the vast, unreasoning and contagious euphoria which traverses the world every New Year's Eve? Or the sympathetic excitement with which we greet the news of a fundamental change in the lives of our friends? A change of partner, a change of occupation, a change of habits, even a change of scene can precipitate against all odds the feeling that henceforth all must go well for the person in question.

This is not the easiest of things to convey in pictorial terms, but I am put in mind of it most vividly by a watercolor which Chagall painted in 1917. He did it more than once, and it is variously titled *The Bridegroom, The Traveler, Forward!* and *Upward and Onward Forever!* (pl. I). It seems to have served as the curtain for a short play by Gogol called *The Wedding,* and Chagall in 1918 planned to use the image on a large scale, out-of-doors, as part of the decorations for the first anniversary of the Russian Revolution in his native town of Vitebsk. So its associations are with adventure and festivity and fulfillment. I know of few pictures which give us so convincingly the sensation of a fresh start in life.

In painting this picture Chagall doubtless had in mind his own situation, which had changed radically since he first came to St. Petersburg in 1907 as a member of a despised minority. At that time and as a Jew he could not even enter the city without a special pass; but by the winter of 1917–18 he was a successful painter with admirers in Paris, in Berlin and in Moscow. He was also a full citizen of his country, and had not long before married a particularly beautiful girl. By the end of 1918 the new regime had installed him as director of the art school in Vitebsk, with jurisdiction over the art life, such as it then was, of the entire province. A year or two later he was painting murals for the Jewish Theater in Moscow. Not only he himself but the whole Jewish community had a fresh start in the new Russia; and he must truly have felt, as the young man in the picture feels, that with one elastic stride he could step over the rooftops and be off and away.

The young man in the picture may of course have expected far too much of a momentary exhilaration. Certainly Chagall's career during the years from 1917 onward was by no means a story of uninterrupted success. In Vitebsk he was outmaneuvered and forced to resign after less than a year in office. Anti-Semitism in Russia was not so much abolished as in abeyance. By 1922 he had given up and gone back to western Europe with 50 years and more of exile before him. His little painting might now seem to stand for an overconfidence more ludicrous than poignant—a last match struck in a hurricane. What was there to be so cheerful about in 1917, with Russia on the edge of famine and civil war, with nearly a million men, French and German, lately killed around Verdun, and with the United States newly committed to a European war?

And yet Chagall's spring-heeled young man really does stand for something that can be traced to the year 1917: the beginnings of a reconciliation between art and society. After about a hundred years in which the two had pulled different ways there was a real chance of their reintegration. Initially the idea of the artist as builder and healer must have seemed ridiculous to those who remembered how for generations art had only to come up with new ideas for society to turn them down flat. (We think of Courbet in jail, Cézanne walled up within his own thoughts, Matisse among the cackling crowds at the Salon d'Automne.) If the people whom Ibsen called "pillars of society" looked to art for confirmation of their importance, they too could count on a rebuff; from Honoré Daumier to George Grosz, art made mock of them. Art and society were in a state of war, declared or undeclared; and even the supposedly safe men, the bemedaled architects and the official portraitists, could not be relied on.

There were exceptions, of course—times when the arts and society worked well together. But it was not through governmental foresight that Henry Hobson Richardson gave a marvelous plain grandeur to the Marshall Field Wholesale Store in Chicago, and when *Harper's Weekly* commissioned wood engravings from Winslow Homer no one at the office knew that the result would capture the quintessence of rural America. When Hector Guimard designed entrances for the Paris subway in 1900 the result was art (fig. 4); but that was not because the city fathers had had art in mind. The posters designed in England in the 1890s by James Pryde and William Nicholson were also art—more so, in fact, than most English paintings of their date—but once again it would be too much to say that the advertisers had planned on getting museum material for their money (fig. 2). What happened from 1917 onward was something quite different—a systematic attempt, all over Europe, to reconcile art with society.

Such things do not happen overnight. The time and the man have to be in collusion, for one thing, and meanwhile the points of departure may pass almost unnoticed. Who would have thought in 1917 that the look of the world would be changed in the end by the publication in neutral Holland, a country then almost phantomatic in its isolation, of a little magazine called *De Stijl?* What possible importance could have been placed on the arrival in Paris of a Swiss architect called Charles-Edouard Jeanneret who had not yet taken the name of Le Corbusier? A notional union of the arts had been much talked about in Ger-

1. Marc Chagall
The Wedding, 1910
Private collection

Chagall was a born storyteller in the great Jewish tradition. If there was little to rejoice in about the everyday life of the Jews in Vitebsk, he responded all the more vividly to exceptional occasions such as the one portrayed here.

2. Beggarstaff Brothers
Rowntree's Elect Cocoa, 1895
The Museum of Modern Art, New York

James Pryde and William Nicholson were brothers-in-law (Nicholson married Pryde's sister, and their son Ben Nicholson became the most famous English painter of his generation), and Pryde's natural sense of drama combined perfectly with Nicholson's deft wit and well-developed sense of characterization. In posters such as this one, even the signature tells.

3. Theo van Doesburg
Composition: The Cow, 1916–17
The Museum of Modern Art, New York

Van Doesburg aimed to reduce the forms of nature to their simplest constituents. Starting from a comparatively naturalistic drawing, he would eat away at the inessentials of the given form until he ended up, as here, with a schema which seemed to him to preserve the fundamentals of the matter while eschewing whatever was merely picturesque.

many before 1914; but with defeat drawing steadily nearer it was hardly likely that the aristocratic patrons of the original idea would be in a position to go on with it. Russia was known to have some gifted painters with a firm grasp of general ideas; but at the moment in November, 1917, when Lenin got control of the entire country it must have seemed the merest fantasy that the new government would have time for such people.

A partisan of the new might, in fact, have made a two-word note in his diary—"conditions hopeless"—at any time, and at almost any place, in the year 1917. But he might also have taken comfort from something said many years earlier by Victor Hugo: "No army in the world can hold out against the strength of an idea whose time has come." When the idea is right, and the man is right, political and social upheavals can do their worst—the idea will make its way. That was what Hugo believed, and history from 1917 onward bore him out.

THE DUTCH EXAMPLE

Nothing great can be done in a hurry, and almost all the people who concern us here had gone through a slow and thorough seasoning by 1917. The magazine *De Stijl* had been thought of as early as August, 1914, by a many-sided near-genius, Theo van Doesburg, who was its animator and ideas man. Already in 1912, at the age of 29, van Doesburg had defined one of the governing principles of *De Stijl*: "Disengage form from Nature," he wrote,

4

4. Hector Guimard
Entrance to Métro Station,
   Paris, c. 1900
Now in the collection of
   The Museum of Modern
   Art, New York

Though now mostly de-
molished in favor of duller
and meaner construc-
tions, Hector Guimard's
elegant and sinuous de-
signs for the Paris subway
were masterpieces of their
kind. Art Nouveau was
here put to practical use,
and hundreds of thou-
sands of Parisians passed
every day beneath an
archway that brought a
luxuriant fantasy to
metropolitan life.

5. Anonymous
Warehouses near New
   Quay, Liverpool,
   Lancashire; 19th
   century

"and what remains is style." What he meant was that the artist should not aim to reproduce—and still less should he aim to rival—the wayward, luxuriant, ever-varying charms of Nature. He should think his way through to the simplest, the fundamental, the irreducible elements of form. Having found them, he should stick with them. It was not his business to imitate, or to ornament, or to tell stories. The question to be asked of his work was not "Is it beautiful?" but "Is it true?"

This was an aesthetic question. Where architecture and design were involved it was also a practical question; but above all it was a moral question. Truth and falsehood, not beauty and ugliness, were the criteria to bear in mind. Truth in architecture meant a style purified of ornament and idiosyncrasy, and one

6. Hans Poelzig
End wall of the
   Chemical Factory in
   Luban, near Posen,
   Germany, 1911–12

Early industrial buildings like the warehouses shown here were remarkable for clarity, directness and freedom from aesthetic pretension. These Liverpool warehouses have a plain grandeur which comes from an absolute truth of intention: the tall, deep-set arches are there not for ornament but to allow goods to be hoisted to the upper stories without blocking the road. Hans Poelzig in 1911–12 had the same kind of intention; nothing in his design is there for effect, but the final result is not far short of sublimity.

II. Theo van Doesburg (in collaboration with
    Cornelis van Eesteren) *Color Construction*,
    1922 (project for a private house)
The Museum of Modern Art, New York

What Mondrian called "equilibrated relationships" were as fundamental to architecture,
in the view of the De Stijl group, as to
everything else in life. "Once we realize,"
Mondrian wrote in 1919, "that equilibrated
relationships in society signify what is just,
then we shall realize that in art, likewise, the
demands of life press forward when the spirit
of the age is ready." Balance was all-
important: van Doesburg and his colleagues
believed that a house should be capable of
being scrutinized, as here, from no matter
how unexpected an angle without being
caught out in a disequilibrated relationship.
They kept, also, to the primary colors—red,
blue and yellow—which were in favor with
Mondrian.

III. Gerrit Thomas Rietveld
Red and Blue Armchair, 1918
The Museum of Modern Art, New York

Rietveld's famous chair is in many ways the
epitome of De Stijl. It is truthful, insofar as form
and function are one, with nothing hidden from
us and nothing elaborated. It keeps to the
primary colors to which Mondrian at that time
restricted himself. And in terms of economy of
manufacture it was (and is) accessible to
everyone.

7. Frank Lloyd Wright
Frederick C. Robie House, Chicago, Illinois, 1909

The Robie House impresses, even today, by the free-flowing rooflines which give a sense of uninterrupted and limitless adventure. Technology had found in Frank Lloyd Wright one of its major poets. A year later he formulated the doctrine which is prefigured in the Robie House: that of the modern building as "an organic entity, as contrasted with the former insensate aggregation of parts."

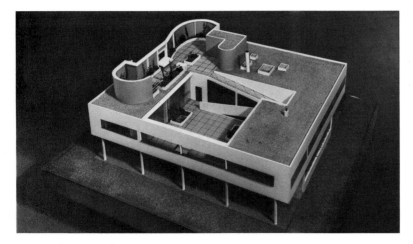

8. Le Corbusier (with Pierre Jeanneret)
Model of the Villa Savoye (1929–31) at Poissy, France
The Museum of Modern Art, New York

The Villa Savoye is, on more than one count, a classic of modern architecture. Where earlier houses sat heavily on the ground, this one stood on legs slender as a gazelle's. Where earlier houses had a front and a back, this one presented itself with equal eloquence in all four directions. Where earlier houses had gardens attached to them at ground level, this one had its garden slung above the living area. The conditions of building and the conditions of living were alike turned upside down.

which declared its function from the outset and used new materials and new building techniques quite openly. Truth in painting meant the end of painting as it had previously existed and the substitution of an art based on equilibrated relationships which owed nothing to Nature.

Van Doesburg shared this point of view with his colleagues in *De Stijl*: the painters Piet Mondrian and Bart van der Leck; the architects J. J. P. Oud, Gerrit Rietveld and Jan Wils; the sculptor Georges Vantongerloo; the designer Vilmos Huszár. It was fundamental to all their activity. But it was not a point of view that they had invented. Already in the 1890s the Belgian painter, architect and designer Henry van de Velde had said that the architecture then in favor was "a lie; all posturing and no truth." The Dutch architect H. P. Berlage, who built the revolutionary Stock Exchange building in Amsterdam in 1898–1903, said much the same thing: the prevailing style was "sham architecture—i.e. imitation, i.e. lying." Berlage went on, "Lying is the rule, and truth the exception. That is why our parents, our grandparents and we ourselves have had to live in surroundings more hideous than any that human beings have known before."

Lying in architecture is the same as lying in life—it means covering up, faking motives, evading, pretending, misleading. As to what form a truthful architecture should take, much was owed before 1914 both to the writings and to the exemplary finished work of an American, Frank Lloyd Wright. As they walked through Paris and Brussels, Berlin and London, European architects could turn in loathing from the fidgety, overblown office buildings that had sprung up on every hand and console themselves with what Wright had had to say: "Simplicity and repose are the qualities that measure the true value of any work of art." Confronted in Wright's own country with the New York Racquet and Tennis Club (an imitation Italian palazzo) or with the domineering portico of the Metropolitan Museum, they could remember what Wright had said in 1910: "The old structural forms, which up to the present time have been called architecture, are decayed. Their life went from them long ago and new conditions industrially—steel and concrete, in particular—are prophesying a more plastic art." The United States had what Europe had not: a plain spoken tradition in architecture and design. If there were such a thing as a North American norm, a common standard to which American design should revert instinctively, it was the tradition of Pennsylvania Dutch barns and Shaker furniture. Such things were truth made visible; and it should be remembered that when a new magazine called *House Beautiful* began publication in Chicago in 1896 it stood for an honest simplification in matters of decoration and design.

But if there was a moral imperative behind all this, there was also—from 1914 onward, especially—a practical one as well. Le Corbusier was a Swiss, and he grew up in La Chaux-de-Fonds in the Jura, which from a cosmopolitan point of view was a long way from anything that mattered. But he had traveled; he had made it his business to get to know the most inventive of living European architects—Josef Hoffmann in Vienna, Auguste Perret in Paris, Peter Behrens in Berlin; and he had taught himself to respond to any given situation by asking himself, "What can architecture do?" As early as 1910 he set down on paper his plans for a new kind of art school; a school strikingly similar, as it turned out, to the one which still had the force of novelty when it was set up by Walter Gropius in Weimar in 1919 and christened the Bauhaus. In the fall of 1914, when most people were still wringing their hands in despair at the destruction to which World War I had already given rise in Flanders, Le Corbusier came up with an idea which, if adopted, would have cut reconstruction time by nine-tenths.

He devised a standard two-story framework, independent of any floor plan, which carried both floors and staircases. Truth, in this context, lay with the methods of the assembly line, the standardized design ingredient, and the mass-produced prefabricated living unit. The architect was no longer restricted to forms that huddled together, as if for warmth, or propped one another up in ways that had hardly varied since the building of Stonehenge. The monolithic, earth-oriented forms of earlier architecture could be discarded, just as single-point perspective was being discarded in painting; as early as 1909 Frank Lloyd Wright's Robie House in Chicago had shown how cantilevering made it possible for forms to fly outward and onward without visible support. Nothing but neurosis could justify continued subjection to such fundamentals of old-style architectural practice as the load-bearing wall, the small fixed window, or the design that was thickest and fattest at the point of its junction with the earth. The time was approaching when houses could be flown in the air on stilts; when inner space could be adjusted at will; when houses need have no front and no back but could be experienced from every point of the compass as fully energized living spaces.

The fundamental prerequisite for all this was that people should acknowledge the truth: that architecture had changed as radically as painting and sculpture, that new materials and new methods of construction should serve new ideas and not old ones, and that the pioneer moves in these directions were manifestations of a collective will to make the world a better, simpler and more rewarding place to live in. It was the *De Stijl* group who got closest, fastest, to this general idea. They knew that painting

9. Piet Mondrian
Self-Portrait, c. 1900
The Phillips Collection,
    Washington, D.C.

Mondrian in private life was a man of almost angelic purity, a high-souled mystic who put up uncomplainingly with a long lifetime of isolation and near penury. Something of this comes out in this self-portrait, which dates from his late twenties.

10. Piet Mondrian
*Red Amaryllis with Blue
    Background*, c. 1907
The Museum of Modern Art,
    New York

In the work of the young Mondrian there were echoes of the Symbolist movement and, also, of van Gogh's sometimes sententious way with still life. A dying sunflower would be turned, for instance, into an image of insistent poignancy. But there were also times when, as happens in this *Red Amaryllis*, Nature looks her finest and firmest; and if the lofty, cruciform image of the lily has mystical overtones it also has affinities with the forms of Art Nouveau glass as it was brought to its point of maximum fulfillment by Louis Comfort Tiffany and others.

9

11. Piet Mondrian
Still Life with Ginger Pot II, 1912
Gemeentemuseum, The Hague

Mondrian first saw the Cubist paintings of Picasso and Braque in the fall of 1911. In May, 1912, he went to live in Paris and set himself to relive, in his own work, the evolution of French painting since Cézanne. (The ginger pot which dominates this painting was a favorite motif of Cézanne's.) Four years after the frantic emotionalism of his *Woods near Oele* of 1908 (pl. IV), Mondrian was concerned with something entirely different: the reduction of still-life material to severe, blocklike forms, with echoes here and there of architecture (see the majestic, portal-like forms to the right of the ginger pot) and of Cézanne's preoccupation with the cube, the cylinder and the cone.

and building could have a great deal in common, and that a house could be very like a sculpture and all the better for it. Theirs was an art of first principles; Mondrian wrote in 1922 that "Theo van Doesburg brought *De Stijl* into being not to 'impose a style,' but to discover and disseminate in collaboration what in the future will be *universally valid.*" Mondrian very much disliked what he called "art as ego expression"; his ambition was to break through to a kind of painting which would make known to everyone the fundamental characteristics of the cosmos. His subject matter was the workings of the universe, not the workings of his own temperament.

He was driven to this in part by the results of his 20 years' investigation of such other forms of art as were current in his day, from Symbolism to Cubism, and in part by the conversation of a new friend, the Dutch philosopher M. H. J. Schoenmaekers, whom he met in Holland in 1914–15. Schoenmaekers was both

mystic and mathematician, and he believed that it was possible, by a process of inner concentration, to arrive at a mathematical understanding of how the universe works. The principles thus established were universally valid and would equip the believer to live in harmony with the universe, with his fellow men and with himself. The truths of art and architecture were intimations of these more general truths. The straight line, the right angle, the alliance of the three primary colors—red, yellow and blue— resulted on this reading from an inspired insight into the nature of the universe. "When beauty was the criterion," van Doesburg wrote, "the undulating line was to the fore. But when truth was the criterion the line simplified itself and will in the end be quite straight."

Cranky as this may have seemed at a time when many laymen still associated good architecture with a superabundance of decoration, it was an idea which soon made its way. For the next 50

IV. Piet Mondrian
Woods near Oele, 1908
Gemeentemuseum, The Hague

As much as Edvard Munch, and as much as his countryman Vincent van Gogh in his more somber moments, Mondrian in his early years would call upon Nature to abet him in the portrayal of states of turbulent emotion. These woods may well remind us of those Scandinavian forests, lit by the unearthly glow of a northern night, into which Munch sent men and women in search of their destiny. It is in a wood such as Mondrian sets before us that the woman in Arnold Schoenberg's opera *Erwartung* stumbles upon the body of her dead lover. What we have here is not the peaceable Dutch countryside but a primeval forest ringed with an unnatural fire: a place of trial and torment, in which a whole generation lived out an important part of its emotional life.

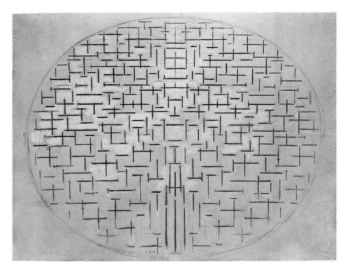

12. (*above left*) Piet Mondrian
Paris Buildings (rue du Depart), c. 1912–13
Sidney Janis Gallery Collection, New York

Before arriving at the schematic presentation of *Blue Façade* (fig. 13), Mondrian made careful notes, as here, of the look of the street in which he lived: the street lamp, the jut and thrust of walls and windows and chimney stacks, and the eye-catching advertisements for KUB and CUSENIER.

13. (*above right*) Piet Mondrian
Blue Façade (Composition 9), 1913–14
The Museum of Modern Art, New York

Living in the Montparnasse district of Paris, and scrutinizing day after day the battered gray façades of the buildings adjacent to his own, Mondrian gradually extracted from them what he needed: a motif in which both verticals and horizontals presented themselves quite naturally, with occasional notes of blue, in the rounded forms of chimney pots, to offset flat, pigeon gray walls and the bright, light-reflecting rectangle of a studio window. *Blue Façade* may look near to abstraction, but everything in it was drawn from direct and daylong observation.

14. Piet Mondrian
Pier and Ocean, 1914
The Museum of Modern Art, New York

At the outbreak of World War I, Mondrian was momentarily in Holland, where circumstances forced him to remain until July, 1919. Looking around for a motif which would allow him to portray visual experience in terms of straight lines that crisscrossed at right angles, he fixed on the look of the North Sea as it lapped against the pier at a neighboring seaside resort. An oval format echoed the Cubist paintings produced by Picasso and Braque in 1912. Except for the firm vertical accent of the pier itself (in the center of the lower edge of the canvas) the painting is dominated by the regular, even, unaccented movement of the sea as it chops back and forth; Mondrian had always enjoyed painting the Dutch coast, and in this case he went beyond the particular to produce a universal image of an enveloping Nature.

years and more the "quite straight" line was the quintessence of modernity. It dominated in architecture, in town planning, in almost every aspect of design. It was accepted as "modern" by people who had never heard of van Doesburg or of *De Stijl*. No one name was attached to it. Insofar as it made its way in painting, however, it was attributed, and quite rightly, to the man who pioneered it and stayed with it: Piet Mondrian.

Mondrian's was, in this sense, an exemplary career. In his art, as in his life, he stood for the cutting away of inessentials. Frugal, solitary and undemanding in his ways, he exemplified one of the key propositions of modern art. In his view, painting should concern itself only with the things that were specifically its own: flat planes laid parallel to the two-dimensional surface of the canvas. His first sojourn in Paris (December, 1911–July, 1914) convinced him that "Cubism failed to accept the logical consequences of its own discoveries; it failed to develop toward the fulfillment of its own ambition, the expression of *pure plasticity*." (By *plasticity* Mondrian meant a picture language which operated on its own, as a closed system, without any descriptive intention.)

He was quite right, of course. Cubism did not develop into abstract art; nor did its founders wish it to do so. It was left to Mondrian to personify the reductive principle: straightening his lines; cutting down his palette to the primary colors—red, blue and yellow; avoiding even the remotest allusion to volume or

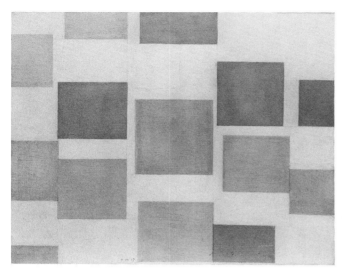

15. Piet Mondrian
Composition with Color Planes, V, 1917
The Museum of Modern Art, New York

Between 1911 and 1917 Mondrian was occupied, as we have seen, with taking an identifiable subject and discarding, one after another, those aspects of it which seemed to him merely incidental. In the Pier and Ocean series both pier and ocean were still present, in however skeletal a form; but there was no pretext in Nature for the pale forms which float in total freedom (so much so that at the top and bottom of the canvas they seem about to move out of sight) in the *Composition with Color Planes, V* of 1917. By 1918 Mondrian was to enclose his rectangles in the thick and usually black lines which were to mark his mature style for many years; but in 1917 Mondrian emphasized the centrifugal, de-focused nature of his composition by allowing them a complete liberty. In this seraphic painting he put forward for the first time in his career an alternative to the taut, focused, centripetal practices of Cubism.

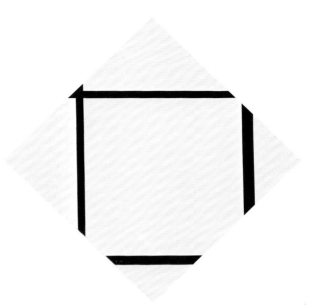

16. Piet Mondrian
Painting I, 1926
The Museum of Modern Art, New York

In devising an art of "equilibrated relationships" Mondrian initially relied on compositions which were both defined and limited by the edges of the canvas. There was no suggestion, in other words, that any of the shapes on the canvas might continue beyond those edges. But in the diamond-shaped *Painting I* it is fundamental to our experience that, three times out of four, the thick black lines should intersect at points beyond the edge of the canvas which are invisible to us. The equilibrium on which Mondrian counted has as much to do with what we cannot see as with what we can; he has cut for us an asymmetrical section from a symmetrical structure, and that asymmetry turns out to have a balance all its own.

recession. He did this not in a dull or doctrinaire way, but at the prompting of an exceptionally full and resonant emotional nature. His pictures were never the same from one canvas to the next. With means which looked meagre he produced a body of work which is rich, strange and surprising beyond all expectation; and he went on developing, as we shall see, until the day of his death.

Straight line and right angle are fundamental to Mondrian's mature work, though no one in our century has used the curved line to more rampageous emotional effect than Mondrian as a young man. Straight line and right angle are the basis, in Holland, of an agriculture which would otherwise soon be under water. They also stand for that element of unyielding puritanism which is basic to the Dutch character; geometry was the basis after all

of the ethical system which was erected in the 17th century by the Dutch philosopher Spinoza. It was natural that when Holland was isolated by her neutral status, the brightest and most ambitious Dutch minds should remain loyal to the traditional armature of Dutch thought. Any student of architecture who has seen a building by Rietveld in Holland will have recognized a reintegration of art and society—the thing needed and the thing done are one. But how much in this success is owed to the clearly defined and sharply characterized nature of the society in question, and to a shrewd assessment of local needs? Would the same principles apply in an unsettled and backward society? Or in quite different climatic conditions? Or in an area which varied enormously in its ethnic ingredients and extended over hundreds of thousands of square miles?

V. Piet Mondrian
Composition C, 1920
The Museum of Modern Art, New York

In 1916–17 Mondrian began to organize his paintings in terms of free-floating rectangles of pure color that slid this way and that across the whole surface of the canvas. From 1917 onward, these rectangles became locked into a mathematical grid and were separated from one another by thick straight lines. The year 1919 saw them set fast in a checkerboard pattern. After his return to Paris in July, 1919, Mondrian allowed himself, as here, both a greater variety in the shapes and sizes of the interlocking rectangles and a new complexity of color: intermediary hues were admitted, where red, blue and yellow had once ruled in their simplest and most uncompromising form.

14

VI. Piet Mondrian
Composition, 1925
The Museum of Modern Art, New York

Mondrian withdrew from the De Stijl group when Theo van Doesburg insisted on reintroducing diagonal elements into his paintings. Possibly it was by way of a reaction to this episode that Mondrian himself was at his crispest in paintings like this *Composition*. With red, blue, black and white, and with no concessions to the complex and relatively suave color structures which he had used a few years earlier, he produced an effect of imperious brilliance.

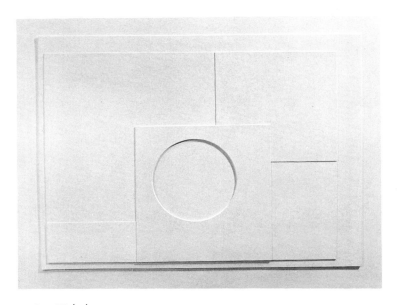

17. Ben Nicholson
White Relief, 1936
Dallas Museum of Fine Arts

Midway between painting and sculpture, and distinguished by the finest
possible sense of placing and balance, the white reliefs of Ben Nicholson made
a contribution all their own to the international modern movement of the
1930s.

18. Gerrit Thomas Rietveld
Schröder House, Utrecht, Holland, 1924

In the Schröder House the balance of forms is as exact as in a painting by
Mondrian or van Doesburg. Even the circular window is placed with an
elegance which foreshadows the white reliefs of Ben Nicholson; and in the use
of materials there is a fastidious regard for contrast and an absolute economy
of statement.

THE RUSSIAN EXAMPLE

These questions are relevant to the situation as it presented
itself to the new rulers of Russia in the winter of 1917–18. It is
one thing to seize power, and quite another to know what to do
with it. Lenin and his colleagues had got the power, beyond a
doubt; but now they had to build, organize and administer a
completely new society. Over the next three years they would be
faced with famine, with a particularly savage and unsparing civil
war, and with bumbling but vindictive interventions by more
than one foreign power. This being so, it is really rather remarkable that from the very day—November 7, 1917—on which
Lenin formed his first government an official role was allotted to
the art of the avant-garde.

A. V. Lunacharsky, himself a poet, a philosopher and a playwright, was put in charge of education and the arts. He had spent
much of his adult life in exile in western Europe; he had a good
working knowledge of the modern movement in France and
elsewhere; above all, he was an enthusiast who saw it as his duty
to make the totality of human achievement freely available to

everyone. "Lunacharsky is drawn toward the future with his
whole being," Lenin said of him. "That is why there is such joy
and laughter in him, and why he is eager to pass on that joy and
laughter to others."

In choosing his collaborators Lunacharsky largely disregarded
political allegiance and went all out for quality. This was not an
outlook which commended itself to the hard liners in the Com-
munist Party, and Lunacharsky often had to compromise, to shift
his ground, to say one thing one day and another the next. But
for three full years, at a time of appalling and ever-worsening
tribulations for Russia and her peoples, he made sure that anyone with something important to offer could count on official
backing. This applied to theater, literature, music, the fine arts
and architecture; for the first and last time the Russian people
were to have free access to the work of their most gifted members.

In matters of art, Lunacharsky could take his pick of a particularly brilliant list of men and women. Some of them had returned

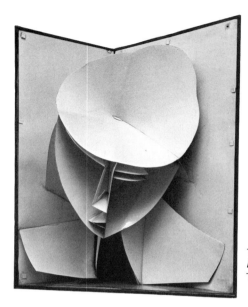

19. Naum Gabo
Head of a Woman, c. 1917–20
The Museum of Modern Art,
New York

It was in 1915–16, when he was living in Norway after several years in Munich and some crucial visits to Paris, that Naum Gabo began to sculpt (or, as he put it, to construct) the human head in terms of opened-out and interpenetrating volumes. What is normally the exposed surface of the head was cut away, in other words, and the head was realized with the use of planes of wood or metal which pushed outward into space. After his return to his native Russia he began to adapt the same principles to transparent materials which made the idea doubly clear.

to Russia at the outbreak of World War I. Nothing in the world is more tenacious than Russian patriotism; and it was this which had brought Kandinsky back from Munich, Chagall back from Paris, and the young sculptor Naum Gabo back from Norway. Others could well have been mentioned earlier in these Volumes as part-time members of the pacific International and long-distance adherents of the cosmopolitan eye. For instance, Vladimir Tatlin had called on Picasso in Paris in 1913 and had been deeply impressed by Picasso's constructions in metal; Kasimir Malevich had exhibited with the Blue Rider group in Munich in 1912; El Lissitzky had lived in Darmstadt (at that time one of the liveliest art centers in Europe), had talked with Henry van de Velde in Brussels, and had walked the length and breadth of Paris in search of what he called "architecture—that is to say, art in its highest sense: mathematical order." As far as architecture in Russia was concerned, the immediately pre-Revolutionary period was distinguished by the erection in Lubyansky Square, Moscow, of a five-story department store, designed by the three Vesnin

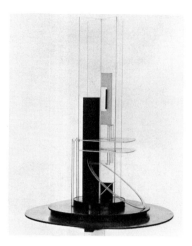

20. (*above left*) Naum Gabo
Column, 1923
The Solomon R. Guggenheim Museum, New York

Gabo was convinced that time, as much as space, would play its due part in the art of the future. Kinetic rhythm, he said, was the basic form in which we perceive what he called "real time"; and in 1920 he attempted to make duration visible in his motorized *Kinetic Construction*, where a metal rod was made to vibrate in such a way as to create an illusion of volume. Later he decided that comparable rhythms would be set up with the use of static materials only; an outstanding instance of this is his *Column*, first mooted in the winter of 1920–21 and later shown all over Europe as a key work in the modern movement. Gabo believed that its principles could be applied not only to works of art but to public buildings; and he made projects of this kind for a radio station, an observatory, an airport and an institute of physics and mathematics.

21. (*above right*) El Lissitzky
Plate 10: *"The New One,"* from the portfolio *Victory over the Sun*, 1923
The Museum of Modern Art, New York

One of the most controversial achievements of the pre-Revolutionary avant-garde in Russia was the opera *Victory over the Sun*, which was produced in St. Petersburg in 1913. The text, music and scenery (the last by Malevich) were all equally daunting to conventional taste; the theme had a prophetic interest in that it described how technology would change the conditions of life by discovering new sources of energy. After the Revolution Lissitzky adapted this same theme for what he called an "electro-mechanical peepshow" or mechanized puppet theater. A portfolio of prints on the same subject, published in 1923, included this classic image of man as he might one day be: alert and indestructible. A mechanized version, in fact, of the young man in Chagall's *Forward!* (pl. I).

22. Vladimir Tatlin
*Project for the Monument
to the Third Interna-
tional,* 1919–20
(reconstruction)

In one or other of its
miniature reconstructions,
Tatlin's projected Monu-
ment has fired the imagi-
nation of young architects
all over the world. Imprac-
tical it may be; but it
triumphs by the sheer
force of its idealism, and
by its refusal to be
daunted by problems of
realization.

23. Mikhail Larionov
*Portrait of Vladimir Tatlin
in Seaman's Blouse,*
1908
Private collection

brothers, in which a reinforced concrete frame did away with the
necessity of structural walls.

It is with human material of this order that Lunacharsky pro-
posed to institutionalize the avant-garde. In normal times this
would have been a contradiction in terms, in that the avant-garde
is by definition outside and ahead of officialdom. But one of the
central facts about Lunacharsky's position in 1917–18 was that
the natural enemies of the avant-garde had simply melted away,
leaving the chairmanships and the professorships and the head-
masterships all empty. "They didn't like us," Naum Gabo said 50
years later, "but they had to put up with us because there wasn't
anybody else." The titles were in any case mainly honorific at
that time: "Being a professor," said Gabo, "simply meant that
you got a little more bread and herring."

Thus it was that Chagall got an important post, and that Kandinsky was given carte blanche in 1920 to redraft the structure
of art education throughout the country, and that Lissitzky got to
design the flag which was carried across Red Square on May Day,
1918. The right flag in the right place is, as we all know, a very
stirring thing; Lissitzky was only one of the artists who made
good use of the new, brief rapprochement between art and society. Interdisciplinary activity flourished in Russia, between 1917
and 1921, in ways not quite paralleled before or since. It is difficult for us to imagine Manet designing a radio station, or Cézanne
making sets for a completely mechanized theater-in-the-round;
but to Lunacharsky's protégés it seemed perfectly natural that the
architect Alexander Vesnin should devise a transparent scaffold-
ing which could be used in a dozen different ways for a production of G. K. Chesterton's *The Man Who Was Thursday,* and that
Naum Gabo should take the delicate colorless membranes which
made up his abstract sculptures and transform them into the out-
line of a radio station which would serve its purpose perfectly.

By no means all of these projects got beyond the stage of the
sketch or the model. Building materials were scarce at that time,
and skilled labor scarcer still, so that many of the more visionary
notions of the Lunacharsky regime had only a faint chance of
realization. The most famous casualty of the period is the *Monument to the Third International* on which Vladimir Tatlin worked
in 1919–20. As planned, this would have been approximately the
height of the Empire State Building. Within a spiral framework of
iron three huge and inhabitable glass forms were to revolve at
varying speeds. The first, a cylinder, would complete its revolution once a year; the second, a cone, once a month; the third, a
cube, once a day. The three glass forms were to be hung on a
dynamic asymmetrical axis in such a way that the building as a
whole would seem to be accelerating into space, moving faster

and faster as the eye followed it upward. The monument was intended to make visible to everyone, on the largest imaginable scale and with all possible versatility, the reintegration of art and society. Quite apart from the inventive magic of the building itself, its functioning would serve as an encyclopedia of the ways in which the poetic imagination of the artist could enrich the life of everyday. Tatlin envisaged the use of giant loudspeakers, for instance, and messages beamed onto the clouds when the weather was bad, and a gigantic cinema screen, clearly visible from below, on which the news of the day would be available to all.

Some of these notions were carried over into the design for the *Pravda* building in Moscow, which was prepared by the Vesnin brothers in 1923–24. They had what may now seem to us an unfounded belief in the impartiality and total openness of the Soviet news services; the *Pravda* building is, in effect, a hymn to transparency. It suggests by implication that *Pravda* has nothing to hide; the elegant inner workings of the Vesnin brothers' design are as open to us as the workings of a specimen watch in a Swiss shop window; the entire building functions as an instrument of communication. Eye, ear and mind were to be seduced in turn; what the Vesnins had on the drawing board was an architecture which would serve up "the truth, and nothing but the truth."

Pravda did not turn out to be that kind of newspaper; nor did the Vesnins' building get built. But if projects like these still haunt our imagination it is because they stand for the hope of a better world in which all the news will be good news and the last of the tyrants will have been shipped off to some maximum-security playpen. Not to have shared at least momentarily in that hope is to have fallen short of our potential as human beings, and it is not surprising that Tatlin's monument has so often been built and rebuilt in scale-model form by architectural students. It symbolizes the fulfillment of the aim which Lunacharsky once set himself—the acceptance at government level of a cultural policy in which everything was possible.

In the conditions then prevailing in Russia it would have been out of the question to initiate an avant-garde of the kind which was already in existence. It was Lunacharsky's good fortune that the people in question not only knew what they wanted to do but in most cases had already been doing it for years. If the political revolution and the aesthetic revolution could work together very closely, for just a year or two, it was not because the one brought the other about. It was because the political revolution had no aesthetic identity and was prepared to settle for whatever lay within reach, just as a man in a hurry to leave for the tropics

24. Vesnin Brothers
Project for the Leningrad "Pravda" Building, 1923–24 (reconstruction)

Transparency is a metaphor, here, for devotion to the truth. Nothing was to be done in this building that would not, in a literal sense, be open to the public. As for the results of it all, they were to be presented in blowups the size of a cinema screen and broadcast through loudspeakers set on high. A dream-newspaper was to be given a dream-building. It was not, unluckily, a dream that was to be transferred into real life.

will buy the featherweight suit that hangs nearest on the rack. There were artists like Tatlin, who genuinely identified himself with Communism and did all that he could to foster its advance; but there were others—Kandinsky, Gabo, Chagall—who were completely apolitical. It is part of the mythology of the period that Lunacharsky's protégés worked together as a band of brothers; but the truth is that if they were brothers it was in the way that Cain and Abel were brothers. Tatlin and Malevich had literally come to blows already in 1915 and never ceased to represent antithetical points of view. Malevich did not scruple to intrigue against Chagall in Vitebsk at a time when Chagall was away in Moscow. Kandinsky's draft plans for the remodeling of art education in Russia were turned down by a majority vote of his colleagues in 1920. Art life in Czarist Russia had always been a ferocious affair, with faction pitted against faction, and all this was if anything intensified after 1917. It was to Lunacharsky's credit that he made no attempt to produce a homogenized official line in such matters, but maintained a watchful impartiality throughout what Naum Gabo has called "the oral period"—the years 1917–20 during which open forums and seminars were

25. El Lissitzky
Model of the set for *I Want a Child* (by Sergei Tretyakov) commissioned by
 Meyerhold for production at his theater in Moscow, 1926–29

Vsevolod Meyerhold, for many years a commanding figure in the world of
Russian theater, had it in mind in the 1920s to open the theater to new social
ideas. Not only would these be acted out on the stage, but the audience
would be free to interrupt the action if they wished, and turn the performance
into an open forum. For this, a new conception of stage design was needed;
and Lissitzky provided this in the context of a play, *I Want a Child*, which dealt
with the problems of a woman agronomist who was bent on having a child
out of wedlock. The text did not find favor with the Soviet authorities and the
production was never realized, but Lissitzky's design remains a pioneer work
in the domain of "total theater."

26. Liubov Popova
Model of the set for *The Magnanimous Cuckold* (by Fernand Crommelynck)
 produced by Meyerhold at the Nezlobin Theater, Moscow, 1922

One of Meyerhold's most dynamic productions in the early 1920s was a farce
by the Belgian playwright Fernand Crommelynck. Set in a windmill and dealing
in the broadest possible way with the discomfiture of a husband who believes
his wife to be irresistible, *The Magnanimous Cuckold* had a transparent,
mechanized set by the painter Liubov Popova, which left the back wall of the
theater in full view of the audience. The wheels, the disk bearing a version of
the author's name, and the windmill sails all revolved at speeds adjusted to
the action of the play. In skeletal form, the set became in turn a bedroom,
a balcony, a machine for grinding flour, and a chute through which sacks of
flour could be discharged.

available in Moscow to an audience totaling in all several thou-
sand. It was in these discussions, rather than in any formal teaching sessions, that ideas were hammered out and tested in debate.

If these things are still worth talking about, it is because so
much of what still passes for the latest thing in the arts was pioneered in Russia at that time. The internal situation of the country
was so desperate between 1917 and 1921 that literally anything
could be tried out on the assumption that Authority was far too
busy to object. If someone wanted to stand on top of the highest
building in the town and conduct a symphony of factory sirens,
he was allowed to do it. If someone wanted to mark a special
occasion by painting not just one big canvas but the whole town,
the project went through unopposed. If street theater with "a
cast of thousands" seemed more the thing, the thousands in
question were drafted. If people in the theater itself—the indoor

one—were bored with the proscenium arch and with the studied
naturalism of plays like Chekhov's *The Cherry Orchard*, they
were encouraged to leave the stage open to the brick wall at the
back of the theater, or to use what Lissitzky called "alogical language" and cast their dialogue in the form of phonetic poems.
If people wanted to paint the trees beneath the Kremlin walls
blue and orange, Lunacharsky let them do it (though Lenin was
not at all amused). If technology put new marvels at the disposal
of the artist, there was no hint of bureaucratic delays; what Lissitzky called a "radio-megaphone" was brought into the theater,
for instance, to allow the audience to be engulfed in "the deafen-
ing noise of railway stations, the rushing of Niagara Falls, the
hammering of a rolling mill." Nothing was allowed to obstruct
the integration of art and society.

And not only could artists do anything, in that brief period of

27. Liubov Popova
Architectonic Painting, 1917
The Museum of Modern Art, New York

Something of the dauntless energy of the age got into this painting, above all in the sharp-pointed arrowlike form that reaches out toward the top left-hand corner of the canvas. In no other country at that time was there a woman painter with quite such a dynamic approach to painting.

tolerance and liberty, they could do *everything* as well. Tatlin could design anything from an exceptionally economical stove to an all-purpose suit of clothing. Malevich took formal elements from his paintings and transformed them into the basis of a new architecture. Alexander Rodchenko was as ready to design a tubular steel chair as to paint an abstract painting—more so, indeed, after 1921, when in common with a number of other painters he moved away from anything that could be called "fine art" and toward the direct service of the proletariat.

Much of all this arose, as I said earlier, from ideas that were in the air all over Europe. But there was also something specifically Russian about it—in the political situation, to begin with, but no less effectively in what can only be called the Russian nature. That nature is distinguished, in a particular context, by a readiness to deal in absolutes of a kind that in most other countries are subject to irony and doubt, an embattled common sense and a readiness to "see both sides." In particular, Russians can move

from the everyday to the mystical without so much as a conversational change of gear. Ultimate problems in most English-speaking countries are thought of as something to be discussed with circumspection and in private. Among Russians they are the staple of human exchange, no more to be skirted than we would expect our butcher to skirt the price of a leg of lamb. Nothing is kept back. Ideas, if held, are held with one's whole being.

All this has been said before by others, but certain things are nonetheless true for being familiar (not least in the novels of Dostoevsky). An individual human nature that is fundamentally oriented toward mysticism will find its way in that direction, no matter how discouraging the circumstances in which it finds itself.

MALEVICH AND THE FUTURE OF PAINTING

The development of Kasimir Malevich, for one, bears this out. Malevich in 1910 was 32 years old. Unlike so many of his colleagues he had never been to western Europe; but from the magazines, and from studying the great French pictures which were freely available to him in the collections of Shchukin and Morozov in Moscow, he knew more than most Frenchmen about what had lately happened in Paris. But when he came to paint the Russian peasant we see what might be called the pawmark of the Russian bear—the heavy, stamping, pounding rhythms that come through so memorably in the Russian dance in *Petrouchka,* which Stravinsky had composed in 1911. Such paintings have a double inspiration: on the one hand, the French Post-Impressionists' use of pure flat color and simplified drawing, on the other the emphatic plain statement of the Russian *lubok,* or popular print.

Malevich's peasant subjects of 1911–12 should, in fact, be related to something that turned up all over the civilized world before 1914—the wish to reinvigorate painting by reference to primitive or demotic modes of expression. Malevich knew a great deal about older European art, but he agreed with the dissident group of painters in St. Petersburg who had said in 1905 that no art of general communication could be fashioned from what they called "a sauce of history." If primeval energies were to hand, they should be tapped; if popular imagery, popular songs, popular forms of narrative were valid for the whole community in ways denied to more sophisticated forms of statement, then they too should be annexed for art. That is what Charles Ives believed when he brought "America the Beautiful" into his Second Symphony, and what Ernst Ludwig Kirchner and his friends believed when they adapted to their own purposes the peremptory black-on-white of the old German woodcut. Malevich had

VII. Kasimir Malevich
Woman with Water Pails: Dynamic Arrangement, 1912
The Museum of Modern Art, New York

VIII. Ivan Puni
Bath, 1915
Private collection

Ivan Puni (who later had a long and successful career in Paris under the name of Jean Pougny) was able, even before the Revolution, to combine avant-garde ideas with down-to-earth social attitudes. With its broad flat areas of unmodulated color, this picture looks forward to the abstract painting of 40 and 50 years later; but by pinning the Russian word for *bath* so bluntly to the surface of the painting Puni reminded his public that the written or printed word could be used simply as a formal element in the picture and with no reference to its meaning in everyday usage.

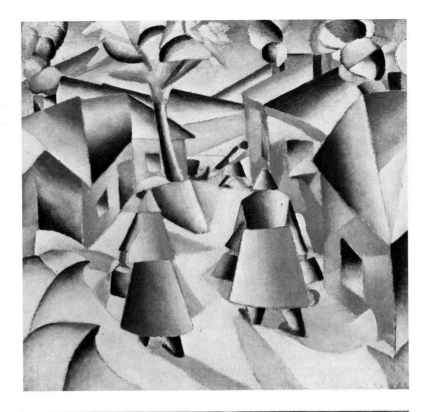

28. (*above left*) Kasimir Malevich
Morning in the Village after Snowfall, 1912
The Solomon R. Guggenheim Museum, New York

29. (*above*) Kasimir Malevich
Private of the First Division, 1914
The Museum of Modern Art, New York

Malevich wanted to annex for himself the formal devices of Cubism, but it was not in his nature at that time to aim for the austere and lucid procedures of Braque and Picasso. He just put in everything—numbers, letters, collaged objects from real life, simulated graining, fragments of printed paper, overlapping flat planes—in the hope that something specifically modern would emerge. Like many another artist in 1914—not least, the American Marsden Hartley—he added some echoes of militarism to make sure that the picture would look well and truly up-to-date

30. (*left*) Kasimir Malevich
Head of a Peasant Girl, 1912
Stedelijk Museum, Amsterdam

Malevich here takes the facts of the human head and rearranges them in folds, much as napkins were once arranged on the dinner table. Curve and cone, firmly modeled in terms of light and shade, were the basic formal elements; but the rearrangement was far more radical than in the two paintings of figures in action which are also shown here (pl. VII, fig. 28).

31. Kasimir Malevich
Suprematist Composition: White on White, 1918?
The Museum of Modern Art, New York

32. Kasimir Malevich
Suprematist Painting,
after 1920
Stedelijk Museum,
Amsterdam

looked closely at Fernand Léger before he painted his *Morning in the Village after Snowfall,* 1912 (fig. 28); but the energizing influence, in formal terms, was that of the *lubok* and of the simplified forms of Russian peasant embroidery.

Malevich in this landscape stressed the look of a little country town after a storm: crisp, delicate, newborn. But he gave unity to his composition by using the same formal ingredient—a cross-section, cut to size, from a cone—for virtually everything in sight: the roofs of the houses, the foliage on the trees, the ups and downs of the village street, the broad back and even broader backside of the woman on the right. This common denominator, shaded in almost every case from left to right and from dark to light, gave an unfailing dynamism to every part of the picture. And eventually it took over from the ostensible subject of the painting to become its true subject—the pulsebeat by which all else was governed.

At a moment which it is now impossible to date, Malevich decided that the pulsebeat of abstract form should be not merely the underlying force within the picture but its only reason for existence. He got nearer to the fulfillment of this idea in a painting of 1912 called *Head of a Peasant Girl* (fig. 30), in which the parts of the head look like starched and folded napkins. Cézanne, a generation earlier, had made his tablecloths look like scaled-down mountain ranges; Malevich in 1912 took the human head— an object which we view with a much greater degree of protectiveness—and gave it, likewise, the stature of a pretext only. But that, too, was a transitional move. Malevich was marking time until he was ready, and until the world was ready, to dispense altogether with recognizable subject matter. In later years he could be very rough with people who still thought that subject matter was essential to art. A painter who delighted in Nature as a subject for art was like a free man who delighted in handcuffs; that was Malevich's eventual point of view, and he went on to make his point with paintings like the famous *White on White* of 1918 (fig. 31).

After well over 50 years these paintings still startle by their total simplification; we have before us a statement that has been pushed as far as it can go by someone who would not settle for anything but the absolute. "In art," said Malevich in 1916, "we need *truth,* not sincerity." He did not mean by this that the artist should not be sincere, but that sincerity on its own could result simply in the perpetuation of obsolete modes of expression. The

25

33. Kasimir Malevich
Suprematist Composition (Airplane Flying), 1914
The Museum of Modern Art, New York

Malevich thought that the airplane had "awakened the soul from its long sleep in the catacombs of reason," and that a new life "somewhere between earth and sky" was waiting for us. Of this new life, the airplane was the true symbol. "Sail forth!" he wrote. "The white free chasm of infinity lies before us!"
To make that visible, he allowed his forms to float freely in a dimensionless ether, like the one indicated here. His object was not to represent any specific airplane, but to confront the observer with an abstract idea of motion in space.

34. Kasimir Malevich
*Suprematist Architectural
Drawing (Future Planits
for Leningrad: The
Pilot's Planit),* 1924
The Museum of Modern
Art, New York

Malevich had great hopes of architecture as a unified and unifying activity, into which both painting and sculpture would one day be incorporated. As a teacher in Vitebsk in 1919–20 he did what he could to encourage young architects to fulfill this notion; in Leningrad, from 1922 onward, he tried to achieve it himself, both in drawings like the one shown here and in three-dimensional models. The general effect of these projected buildings was as if the forms which float through the air in Malevich's Suprematist paintings had been allowed to settle on the ground, with their recent passage through space plotted in three dimensions.

sympathetic observer was back with the notion of truth, just as he was back with it in western Europe and back with it in the Chicago of Frank Lloyd Wright; truth meant defining the quintessence of the painting experience. When Malevich put a black square in the middle of a white canvas he meant the square to stand for sensation and the white surround to stand for the blank state of awareness and expectation on which sensation impresses itself. Even that came to seem to him too obvious, and in the *White on White* painting, first shown in 1919, color dropped out altogether; sensation and its surround merged into one another, distinguished only by a change of texture and by the spectral pivoting of a white square which hovered, weightless, within the confines of a larger square of its own color.

We may feel, in common sense terms, that such paintings give us nothing to look at. But Malevich took exactly the opposite point of view. In his Suprematist pictures (as he called them) there is, for the first time in the history of art, nothing to distract or deceive. The experience comes to us pure and entire. The square on a square, thus interpreted, stands for primary, irreducible emotional structure: the power to set one element in our experience against another, and to define the relationship between them. These paintings provide, in other words, a schema or pilot system which helps us to find our way among our own feelings. Malevich and Kandinsky did not always see eye to eye; but fundamentally Malevich was carrying on with the mystic or intuitional line of thought which Kandinsky had pioneered in his book *On the Spiritual in Art.* Once again, and without falling back on any stereotyped view of the Russian nature, one could say that the speculations of both men had an all-or-nothing character, a compulsive inwardness, and a disdain for ridicule which are not common in other countries. The square, the circle and, to a lesser degree, the triangle are fundamental to much of the abstract painting of the last 50 years; but nobody has quite felt about the square in the way that Malevich felt about it, any more

IX. Kasimir Malevich
Suprematist Composition, 1916–17?
The Museum of Modern Art, New York

than anyone has felt about the circle in the way that Kandinsky did in the 1920s. ("If I have used the circle so often and so passionately in the last years," he wrote in 1929, "it is not because of the geometrical shape of the circle, or of its geometrical attributes, as because of my overwhelming recognition of its inner strength and its limitless variations.")

Malevich did not think of these paintings as objects of luxury to be sold to the highest bidder. Still less did he regard them as addressed to a cultivated elite. He thought of them as terminal statements. If they signaled the end of art as it had previously been known—if "art," thus understood, was a casualty of evolution—that seemed to him a perfectly fair exchange for the new spirituality which his paintings made available to everyone. Those simplified flat shapes afloat on a plain background stood, in his eyes, for the new life that was opening up for the human spirit. And the coming of that new life was overdue. "Their bodies may fly in airplanes," he said of his contemporaries, "but they live by the beauty of ages long past."

The Malevich who wrote those words was not a peripheral crank to whose ravings no importance was attached. He had established himself among his fellow artists as early as December, 1915, as a leader with whom it was rash to quarrel. Nor was he a man to put his head in the clouds by way of escape from the realities of life after 1917. He saw nothing contradictory in calling on the one hand for a new and exalted degree of spirituality, and in promoting on the other a future bound up with automated, electrified and prefabricated housing. It may seem that at a time of extreme national emergency the one might have precluded the other. But that is to misunderstand what Edmund Wilson in *A Window on Russia* called "the Russian perception of time—a sense of things beginning, of things going on, of things to be completed not at the present moment but in the future, of things that have happened in the past all relegated to the same plane of pastness with no distinction between perfect and pluperfect: a sense, in short, entirely different from our Western clock time, which sets specific events with exactitude in relation to an established and unvarying chronology."

Our Western clock time did catch up, even so, both with Malevich and with Lunacharsky's regime as a whole. By the end of 1921 Lunacharsky's policy of humane tolerance had been dismantled in favor of a program which admitted only those forms of art which had an immediate social utility. A Russia in which anything was possible gave way, step by step, to a Russia in which nothing was possible. To have some idea of the personal suffering which was inflicted on people who had much to give to the world, the reader should turn to the poems of Anna Akhmatova

35. (*above*) Marcel Breuer
Whitney Museum of American Art,
    New York, 1963–66

36. (*below*) Ludwig Mies van der
    Rohe
Lounge Chair ("Barcelona" Chair),
    1929
The Museum of Modern Art,
    New York

and Nadezhda Mandelstam's two volumes of memoirs, or to those many compositions in which Shostakovitch turns a bleak and unforgetting eye upon the ordeals of his generation. What we are concerned with here is something quite different: the continued existence in other countries, and into other decades, of that same pacific International which had been active before 1914, and of which the Lunacharsky regime was a distinguished and highly localized offshoot. It was thanks to this pacific International, and to the extreme receptivity of its most prominent members, that the contribution of Russia between 1917 and 1921 should be seen not as an isolated and foredoomed experiment, but rather as one episode in an ongoing process that made itself felt all over Europe in the 1920s and later spread to the United States.

THE BAUHAUS EXAMPLE

As early as 1910, when he was in his late 20s, Walter Gropius was arguing that aesthetic creativity and industrial mass-production were perfectly compatible. Noting how in the United States Thomas Edison had made extensive use of poured concrete and standard components made of iron, he foresaw a time when the bricklayer and the carpenter would play no part in architecture. In 1911 his factory for the shoe-last firm of Fagus proved that exterior walls need no longer bear heavy loads and could, on the contrary, be no more than transparent shields against the weather. Even in the worst days of World War I Gropius went on planning for a school that would synthesize the arts and the crafts and see to it that the best ideas of the age were made available cheaply and to everyone. Himself a Berliner, he would have preferred to have a school in Berlin, one of the great capitals of the world, rather than in Weimar, a small country town best known for its associations with Goethe, Schiller, Liszt and Nietzsche. It is one of the ironies of history that the Bauhaus, which was finally dreamed up in a Berlin on the very edge of a proletarian revolution, should have its first home in a set of buildings designed in 1904 by Henry van de Velde at the request of the Grand Duke of Saxony.

Between 1919 and 1933 the Bauhaus had on its staff, at one time or another, as brilliant a group of men as ever taught. The New Yorker who wishes to realize the extent of their radiation has only to walk around midtown Manhattan. The Seagram Building is by Mies van der Rohe (Bauhaus, 1930–33) and Philip Johnson; the Whitney Museum is by Marcel Breuer (Bauhaus,

37. Herbert Bayer
Kandinsky zum 60. Geburtstag (Kandinsky's 60th Birthday), 1926
The Museum of Modern Art, New York

After half a century Herbert Bayer's graphic designs of the mid-1920s still look specifically modern. Bayer was a pioneer communicator, who aimed to bring new life to advertising with the help of moving pictures, the public-address system, electric lights that told a story and, in one instance, a column of smoke that spelled out a message.

38. (*below*) Jan Tschichold
Buster Keaton in: "Der General"
The Museum of Modern Art, New York

39. Lyonel Feininger
Cathedral, 1919
The Museum of Modern Art,
New York

The inaugural program of the Bauhaus was written by Walter Gropius in April, 1919. "We must all return to the crafts!" was its theme; and although Gropius looked forward to "the new structure of the future" which was to "rise toward heaven from the hands of a million workers like the crystal symbol of a new faith," the structure which appeared on the program itself was of purely medieval inspiration.

40. Oskar
Schlemmer
*Study for "The
Triadic Ballet,"*
1922
The Museum of
Modern Art,
New York

1920–28); the Pan Am Building above the train shed at Grand Central Station is by Walter Gropius (Bauhaus, 1919–28) and his partners. The collection of the Solomon R. Guggenheim Museum is dominated by Wassily Kandinsky (Bauhaus, 1922–33). It is difficult to go into an office that calls itself modern and not find chairs designed at the Bauhaus by either Breuer or Mies. In a more general way, Moholy-Nagy (Bauhaus, 1923–28) produced a revolution in communications techniques, and Herbert Bayer (Bauhaus, 1921–28) a revolution in graphic design, which still influence every American who wants to get a message across. Generations of American students owe much to the painter Josef Albers (Bauhaus, 1920–33), who began teaching at Black Mountain College in 1933 and was teaching classes at Yale as recently as 1960. Not merely the example but the name of the Bauhaus crossed the Atlantic when, in 1937, Moholy-Nagy founded The

New Bauhaus: American School of Design (since 1939 The Institute of Design) in Chicago. It would be fair to say that American life is permeated by the influence of the Bauhaus and that even those who have never heard of the original school have had reason to be grateful to it.

This is not to say that the history of the Bauhaus was either consistent or glorious. There were changes of internal policy, changes of personnel, changes of orientation. Though outwardly nonpolitical, the school depended for its existence on support from whatever party was in power; the times were turbulent, as often as not, and things were done which would not have been done had the school been functioning with ample funds in a stable society. Internal disputes set individual against individual, and discipline against discipline. Sometimes students complained that they did not see their famous teachers for months

42. Walter Gropius
The Bauhaus, Dessau, 1925–26

The Bauhaus in Dessau was designed by Gropius, but in certain respects it was the work of a Bauhaus collective: the furniture was designed by Marcel Breuer, for instance. Gropius also took into account the presence in Dessau of the Junker aircraft factory. "Air traffic routes demand," he said, "that architects should design their buildings to be seen from the air in ways that until lately were unthinkable."

41. Oskar Schlemmer
Bauhaus Stairway, 1932
The Museum of Modern Art, New York

Oskar Schlemmer's activity was fundamental both to the sculpture workshop at the Bauhaus and to its theatrical ventures. His experiments in the field of ballet can still be reconstructed with hallucinatory impact. Something of their effect—part sculptural, part humanized robot—can be judged from Schlemmer's paintings. In this particular one, the upward movement of students on the main staircase of the Bauhaus can be read symbolically: a new world lies on the next landing.

on end. A regime which aimed at the updating of the medieval guild system would be followed by one which crossbred lectures on Gestalt psychology with compulsory physical training. It is easy to speak ill of a school which aimed in 1919 to "build the cathedral of Socialism," only to peter out in August, 1933, with the announcement that it was closing down not because of any reluctance to make concessions to the Nazis but because it simply hadn't the money to go on.

Yet the indispensable thing in the 1920s was to keep the Bauhaus in being as a laboratory in which ideas of every kind could be tested in practice, from the prototype of a mass-produced house (summer, 1923) to the experimental ballets devised by Oskar Schlemmer (Bauhaus, 1920–29). The Bauhaus propositioned the future continually. Already in the mid-20s Gropius was experimenting with new forms for architecture that would be seen to best advantage from the air; Ludwig Hirschfeld-Mack (Bauhaus, 1920–27) was encouraged to "make the immaterial visible" in his reflected-light compositions with musical accompaniment; on the level of the everyday, anyone who wanted a Bauhaus wardrobe, a Bauhaus letterhead, a length of Bauhaus

43. László Moholy-Nagy
Light-Space Modulator, 1923–30
Busch-Reisinger Museum, Harvard University, Cambridge, Mass.

Moholy-Nagy believed that the manipulation of light would one day be one of the most eloquent of all the techniques which art has at its disposal. He envisaged projections onto clouds, three-dimensional displays of colored light through which the spectator was free to walk, and even more grandiose light spectacles which would be viewed from a seat in a specially chartered airplane. Light and color would not merely make use of space with a new freedom; they would remake and remodel space in ways never before dreamed of. This mobile *Light-Space Modulator* was a first start in these directions.

44. László Moholy-Nagy
Nudes on the Grass, 1929
(photograph)
The Museum of Modern Art, New York

Moholy-Nagy pioneered, among so much else, the notion of making negative prints from positive transparencies to produce an image which both recalled and contradicted our everyday experience. The reclining human body took on, as here, a look of jointed marble; human hair seemed turned to flame, and individual blades of grass were picked out as if by an etcher's needle.

fabric or a roll of Bauhaus wallpaper could count on finding one. The Bauhaus was meant to cover the whole spectrum of human activity, from the loftiest and most spiritual to the plain and down-to-earth, and from handcrafting and Oriental mysticism to electronic music and the six-screen cinema. It was for this reason that when the school was in danger in 1924, an international committee was formed to support it; science was represented on that committee by Albert Einstein, music by Arnold Schoenberg, painting by Marc Chagall and Oskar Kokoschka, architecture and design by the veteran pioneer Josef Hoffmann. These people knew that the Bauhaus was invaluable to a convalescent Europe, and that for all its internal divergences and contradictions it wanted to give everyone, everywhere, a better life.

As to just what that better life should be like, the version in favor varied from year to year. (It seems likely, for instance, that

45. Wassily Kandinsky
Composition 8, 1923
The Solomon R. Guggenheim Museum, New York

Kandinsky returned to Germany from Russia late in 1921. He became a founding member of the Bauhaus faculty in 1922 and taught there until the school was closed in 1933. In this very large painting he mingled the slender, free-flying diagonals which had been developed in Russia by Malevich with forms of his own preference: above all, the circle. The image as a whole was not one of chaos barely held in check, as had been the case with Kandinsky before 1914; it was characterized by clear-cut forms and a look of exact calculation.

the Bauhaus authorities were none too pleased when Theo van Doesburg arrived in Weimar in 1921 and set up public classes of his own.) Johannes Itten (Bauhaus, 1919–23) was the author of the first version of the foundation course which all students had to take; but his mixture of esoteric wisdom with the wearing of specially designed robes and a mandatory Bauhaus diet with quadrupled garlic ration was too much for his colleagues, and Itten was replaced in 1923 by László Moholy-Nagy. Moholy-Nagy was a one-man compendium of the postwar pacific International. He had shared a studio with Kurt Schwitters, he had attended the Constructivist Conference which had been called by van Doesburg in Weimar in 1922, he knew Lissitzky, he was familiar with the achievement of Malevich. By the time he arrived in Chicago as a refugee in 1937 he had distinguished himself as painter, filmmaker, stage designer, kinetic sculptor, photogra-

46. Paul Klee
The Hopeless Ones, 1914
Marian Willard Johnson, New York

Time was running out for the old order in Europe when Paul Klee painted this little picture not long before the outbreak of World War I. For all its characteristic modesty of scale it gives us most vividly a sense of civilization gone out of control, and of the incapacity of individual human beings to master destiny.

pher, editor, book designer, cultural historian, poster maker, interior designer, and above all as one of this century's great teachers.

It may, in fact, be Moholy-Nagy in the end who most thoroughly validates the Bauhaus' reputation for modernity. By the second half of the 1920s people were already remarking on the fact that the school was dominated by people whose careers had begun before 1914, and that a manifesto prefaced by a woodcut of a Gothic-style cathedral had always augured oddly for an institution which prided itself on being up-to-date. With Moholy-Nagy, no such complaints were possible. He, if anyone, was alert to all the possibilities of his time. (In 1922 he had painted a picture by telephone, giving orders so exact that they could be carried out by any skilled executant.) In his books *The New Vision: From Material to Architecture* and *Vision in Motion* an attentive reader will find a running fire of ideas and injunctions as to how best to bring about the reintegration of art and society.

Moholy-Nagy said in 1922 that "the art of our century, its mirror and its voice, is Constructivism." In this he followed Lissitzky, Gabo and Tatlin, all of whom were convinced that new materials called for a new art, and a new art which would above all be

X. Paul Klee
Building the L-Platz, 1923
Kunstsammlung Nordrhein-Westfalen, Düsseldorf

Klee knew everything there was to know about how to make a picture: what codes to use, how to combine them, when to surprise the observer and when to ease him back onto familiar ground. As a teacher at the Bauhaus he made all this available to his students. But there remained something that could be neither taught nor learnt: the imaginative energy which Klee possessed in the highest degree. *Building the L-Platz* is, on one level, as flat as the map which it pretends to be: "B" and "C" stand for adjacent areas on that map, the word "Plan" drives the message further home, and the designation "L-Platz" marks out a space on which nothing will be built. Klee has drawn in the roads which meet at the L-Platz, and the houses, the church and the railroad tracks which form part of the scene. Sometimes they are in diagram form; sometimes they are realized in depth, as happens with the treelined road in the center. The picture pulls several ways, and the wiry but strictly evocative drawing is offset by patches of color which harmonize in ways unrelated to the principal image.

XI. Paul Klee
Fire in the Evening, 1929
The Museum of Modern Art, New York

When Klee went to Egypt in the winter of 1928–29 he was deeply impressed by the patterns of Egyptian agriculture: long strips of tilled land, precisely parallel to one another but varying in width, with here and there an irrigation channel to offer a contrast both of color and of texture. On his return to Europe he completed a series of pictures which derived from this experience. Some of them bore titles like *Upper Egypt,* or *Monument on the Edge of Fertile Country,* which made the reference doubly clear. Others "moved far from

Nature"—in Klee's own words—"and found their way back to reality." Among the latter, *Fire in the Evening* is the finest. There is nothing directly illustrative about it, but the rectangle of brilliant red, just right of center, stands out as a fire would stand out in the far distances of the Nile Valley. In the foreground, below, are browns and greens, colors of earth and vegetation, hooded by the onset of the night; at the top, unbroken bands of pink and blue stand for the last flaring of the light. The point of departure was the stratified look of Egyptian agriculture; but from that point onward Klee felt free to find his own way back to reality.

47. Paul Klee
The End of the Last Act of a Drama, 1920
The Museum of Modern Art, New York

Klee loved the theater in all its aspects, from the homemade marionettes which he once produced for his small son to the sweep and splendor of great actors at full stretch. He once likened the last scene of Mozart's opera *Don Giovanni* to the moment after a thunderstorm when "people look out of the window to see who's still alive"; and in this picture he portrays a moment of that sort, with the body of the main character laid out across the length of the foreground and the rest of the company standing silent and aghast. Only the cat (on the right) and the sun and the moon in the sky go about their business as usual.

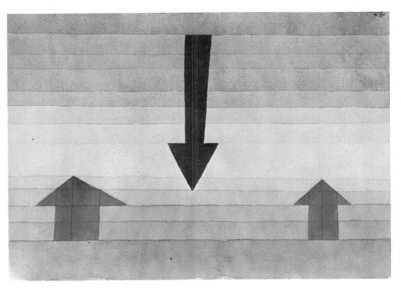

48. Paul Klee
Begrüssung (Greeting), 1922
Wadsworth Atheneum, Hartford, Conn.

Klee's paintings look sometimes as if they had been dreamed up more or less at random. But in point of fact he took immense pains with their coded language. The arrow sign, for instance, has always an exact meaning when Klee employs it; and in this picture, in the simplest possible manner, he shows us what happens when three people meet and one of them goes out of his way to welcome the others. With the strong downward thrust of the upper arrow and a significant deepening and darkening of the color, we get the message loud and clear.

dynamic and kinetic in its allegiances; a clean break was to be made with the static apartness of older art, and with its traditional stance on wall or floor. There was inevitably some conflict of direction between the teaching which set out this point of view and the teaching of Wassily Kandinsky, Paul Klee (Bauhaus, 1920–31) and Lyonel Feininger (Bauhaus 1919–33); these three were "fine artists" in the traditional sense insofar as their end product was predominantly an oil painting on canvas. Kandinsky at one moment was influenced by the Constructivist work which he had seen in Russia, and in particular by the hovering in space of apparently weightless flat forms which he had seen in paintings by Malevich. But basically he was still preoccupied with states of being rather than with the potential of technology; and as far as the Bauhaus was concerned he regarded the inclusion of his ideas as fundamental to the mix. Mies van der Rohe told Kandinsky in September, 1932, that as director of the Bauhaus he meant to curtail, if not actually abolish, the art classes in the school. Kandinsky wrote back that every student had the right to rediscover those inward links with Nature which had been lost for centuries. Dependence on the outward look of Nature was more and more a thing of the past in painting; what modern art called for, and what Kandinsky tried to provide, was the spiritual element: "Not the shell, but the nut," as he himself put it. The art classes were kept on.

With Paul Klee there was also no question of a blanket rejection of the past, or of a surrender to new materials from which new magic might or might not be conjured. "Klee taught us," one student wrote later, "to see the composition and structure

49. Paul Klee
Pastorale, 1927
The Museum of Modern Art, New York

All systems of notation fascinated Paul Klee. In *Pastorale* he mimicked the look of an incised tablet, covered it with forms of the kind that are universal among doodlers, and yet ended up with a painting that exactly evokes the open arches of North African architecture, the carefully cultivated strips of land that have to be coaxed into growing anything at all, the spiked forms of trees and (at the very top) a sliver of pale blue to stand for the sky.

of animal and vegetable life. Not only did he teach us to perceive it visually, but in his theory of forms he taught us the principles of creativity. He showed us the all-encompassing synthesis which embraces all life, whether organic or inorganic. Everything—zoology, biology, chemistry, physics, astronomy, literature, typography—helped us to understand how with every bit of our existence and every one of our activities we are part of humanity and part of the rhythm of the cosmos."

It will by now be clear that the Bauhaus was too complex and too variable an institution to be epitomized in a few sentences. But at its best it was powered by the fresh-start syndrome to which I referred initially. Whether it was Gropius with the transparent, wraparound design for the new Bauhaus building in Dessau, or Moholy-Nagy with his plans for the projection of cinematic images onto clouds of tinted vapor, or Kandinsky and Klee rethinking the pictorial process from the first dot onward, there was a determination to begin again from the beginning. It was an international and collective adventure, which allied gifted Berliners, with their inborn sense of emergency and openness to ideas from all over, to a Russian, a Swiss, and a Hungarian, as well as to ideas first mooted by Dutchmen.

LEGER AND METROPOLIS

From this concert of the nations one great European voice was lacking, however; France contributed nothing to the Bauhaus, and it would hardly be an exaggeration to say that the Bauhaus might as well have been in Kamchatka for all the impact that it made on French thinking and French life.

There were several good reasons for this. French life, unlike German life, had not been brought to a near standstill at the end of World War I. The fundamental re-analysis for which the Bauhaus stood had no appeal in France, where it was taken for granted that the best art had been made in Paris and would go on being made there until the end of time. The best and brightest natures in France were not, on the whole, preoccupied with the making of a new society; nor was the old society disposed to let them try. The French were complacent, but they had a great deal to be complacent about: not least, a life style which, as visiting Americans saw for themselves, was uniquely agreeable. Men and women were left alone to be themselves, in France in the 1920s, with a civilized discretion which it would be hard to parallel today.

So the idea of the fresh start did not have too many attractions in France. At a time when Monet was still alive, and when Matisse, Braque, Picasso, Bonnard and Max Ernst were in full

50. Fernand Léger
The Mechanic, 1920
The National Gallery of Canada, Ottawa

51. Fernand Léger
The City, 1919
Philadelphia Museum of Art

output, the case for starting again all over—in art, at any rate—
was really very weak. But there was one major artist who did,
even so, propose to reformulate the relationship between art and
society, and that artist was Fernand Léger. As we have already
seen, Léger as a soldier in World War I formed social allegiances
which were remote from those of the moneyed man of taste.
There was nothing exclusive or doctrinaire about these allegiances—he was delighted, for instance, to make friends with the
American expatriates Gerald and Sara Murphy, and through them
to sample the world which was memorialized by F. Scott Fitz-
gerald in *Tender Is the Night;* but it seemed to him self-evident
that a new kind of art and a new kind of man should go together.
And in a painting called *The Mechanic* of 1920 (fig. 50) Léger
gave that new kind of man the treatment that painters reserved
in earlier times for the great ones of the earth—he made him
immortal, in other words.

   The Mechanic is so compelling, so absolutely true to one particular moment in time, that it puts the social historian out of
business. Here is the archetypal French working man for whom
the machine might still prove to be an instrument of social libera-
tion. He is seen in profile, like the kings and queens on their gold

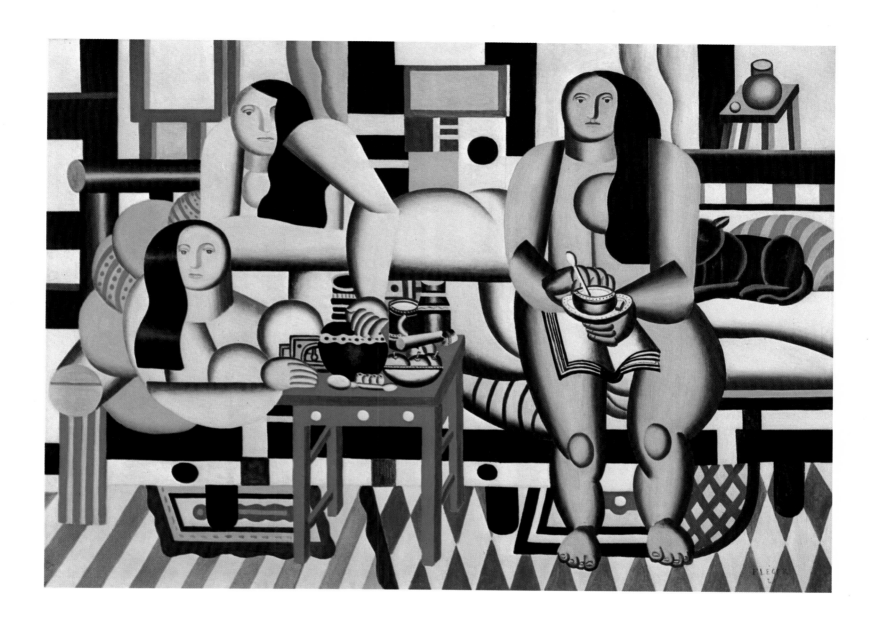

XII. Fernand Léger
Three Women (Le Grand Déjeuner), 1921
The Museum of Modern Art, New York

52. Le Corbusier
Still Life, 1920
The Museum of Modern Art, New York

In 1918 Le Corbusier and his close friend Amédée Ozenfant produced a book which was called *After Cubism.* Harmonious proportion was to be the basis of post-Cubist painting, with a strict attention to vertical motifs, which stood for dynamic power, and horizontal ones, which stood for repose. Order, control, precision and equilibrium were to be the master qualities of the new painting; the fugitive, the whimsical, the transient and the ambiguous were outlawed.

and silver coins. With his nautical tattoo, his sleeked-down hair and his heavy mustache, his cigarette in full combustion and a pair of rings on his well-fleshed third finger, he stands for the belief that the life of the industrial masses need not be without dignity, nor the individual mass-man become a disinherited cipher. He is neither heroicized nor sentimentalized, but seen for what he is: a man with a mind of his own, who is at one with his machines and could ask no greater fulfillment than to be in charge of them.

In this painting, and even more so in the panorama called *The*

City of 1919 (fig. 51), Léger presented the new metropolitan scene as an earthly paradise: a place of bright, flat color, simplified machine forms, and staircases that climbed straight into the sky. No such city existed, but Léger hoped that his paintings would help to bring one about. Nor did his optimism exceed the bounds of practicality. He never pretended, for instance, that the role of the human being in the new city would be anything but subordinate. The human being was shown as an object among other objects: a color note, or an abstract, simplified volume. He was not individualized—except when, as happens in *The Mechanic,* he was off duty and could smoke a cigarette. But neither was he diminished by his objecthood: rather, it raised him to the level—that of a functional elegance, a stripped-down beauty independent of hierarchical precedent—that was the mark of every other element in the new metropolitan scene.

These were not undertakings in which Léger could hope for support from his French contemporaries; but they did commend themselves, very much indeed, to the members of the De Stijl group. Piet Mondrian was living in Paris from 1919 onward; he had written enthusiastically about Léger in an early issue of *De Stijl,* and it seems likely that the background of *The Mechanic* was prompted by van Doesburg's paintings and, even more, by Mondrian's insistence on the power of the straight line to equilibrate even the most complicated subject matter. In 1920 Léger also made friends with the architect who came nearest to realizing his dream of the new metropolis—Le Corbusier. Le Corbusier in 1925 gave Léger his first mural commission, and in 1928 Léger returned the compliment by giving a lecture on Le Corbusier in Berlin.

Léger also differed from Matisse and Braque in that he looked about him for aspects of modern communications systems which could be annexed for painting. *The City* is, for instance, on the scale of the movie screen; Léger had been keenly interested in the movies since Apollinaire took him to a Chaplin program in 1916, and in the year after he painted *The Mechanic* he collaborated on a film called *La Roue* with that pioneer of the epic film, Abel Gance. *The City* can be read as an anthology of cinematic method at the time, with its abrupt changes of scale and focus, its rapid crosscutting from one image to another, its purposeful singling out of incidents which in everyday life might seem trivial or escape notice altogether. (In 1924 Léger made a film of his own, the storyless *Ballet Mécanique,* with the American cameraman Dudley Murphy. In this, as in his paintings of the same date, he took objects of everyday use, abstracted them from their normal contexts, and banished all attempts at "atmosphere" and all references to Nature or the human body, and by the skillful use of crosscutting, repetition and rhythmic emphasis was able to give the objects in question a planned and calculated identity of an entirely new sort.)

What Léger had in mind at this time was an aesthetic of concern: a scale of values which would admit to the canon of beauty such manifestations of the new age as the Motor Show, the Aviation Show, the Boat Show, the neon sign, the cross section of a spark plug and—yes, why not—the soda syphon. The ultimate ambition of the aesthetic of concern was that every man and every woman should feel part of "an unhurried, peaceful and well-regulated society, in which Beauty is in the natural order of things and need neither be gushed over nor romanticized."

In this, Léger was at one with his friend Le Corbusier, and at one with Amédée Ozenfant, the teacher and theorist with whom Léger was to set up a school in 1924. Le Corbusier had in many ways a middle-class orientation—"in a decent house," he wrote in 1926, "the servants' staircase does not go through the drawing room"—but he did nonetheless envisage a classless aesthetic of construction, one in which houses would go up all in one piece, "assembled the way Henry Ford assembles cars," and "built like an aircraft, with the same structural methods, lightweight framing, metal bracers and tubular supports." In this, as in so many pronouncements of the period immediately after World War I, the syndrome of the fresh start is fundamental. And the best way to make a fresh start, so it then seemed, was to define the irreducible essentials and begin again from there.

Here the painter had the advantage over the architect. The architect needed a patron and could be betrayed by him not only while he was building the house but at any time after it was finished; the painter had complete control over his canvas. He could not compel anyone to look at it, but at least he alone was in charge. Le Corbusier had so many unhappy experiences in his architectural career—projects scorned and derided, projects acclaimed but unfulfilled, projects completed but later degraded by their inhabitants—that he set what often seemed an exaggerated value on his activity as a painter. Neither he nor Ozenfant wished to seduce in their paintings. "The aim of pure science," they wrote in 1919, "is to express natural laws through the search for constants. The aim of serious art is, likewise, the expression of invariants." The work of art thus arrived at should, in their view, be "generalized, static, and expressive of the invariant." An absolutist outlook of this sort is often modified in practice, but Ozenfant and Le Corbusier were not the men to waver; and their paintings had almost always, and not surprisingly, a look of the drawing board.

They are important to us, even so, and not least because we

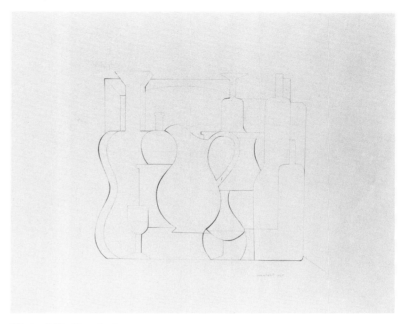

53. Amédée Ozenfant
Fugue, 1925
The Museum of Modern Art, New York

Amédée Ozenfant was never a painter of the first rank, but he applied himself to the problems of how to paint in the machine age with a rare lucidity and an exceptionally wide range of background information. It was from his writings, in particular, that more than one generation both in Europe and the United States learned of the new range of options which was open to art. In paintings such as this one, Ozenfant took as his subject matter objects of everyday use that were (in his own words) "so banal as hardly to have an existence of their own"; impersonal expression was to be applied to impersonal objects.

can learn from them how rich and various, by comparison, was Léger's creative nature. Beside the severe and careful distillations of Ozenfant and Le Corbusier, Léger's *Three Women* of 1921 (pl. XII) is the work of a born painter who can recreate the monumental structures of the European past in terms of the new art, the new technology, and the new styles of living which the third decade of the 20th century had already brought into being. Léger liked to present himself as the spokesman of the industrial working man (though in point of fact he was the son of a prosperous cattle-breeder and had never done a day's work in a factory), and

in his published writings he never stressed his knowledge of the French classical tradition. But, just as Naum Gabo said that "the history of Russian art had more influence on our generation than Cubism, Futurism and all the rest of the Western ideologies put together," so there is often behind Léger's most down-to-earth compositions a discreet echo of the brothers Le Nain, who proved with their studies of peasant life in the 17th century that there need be no such thing as a social hierarchy when human beings are taken as the subject matter of great art.

Léger had worked in an architect's office, and he had a great architect, Le Corbusier, for his close friend and colleague. He liked to introduce into his paintings what was in effect an ideal architecture. This was a matter of forms reduced to an ultimate simplicity: a horizontal plane, or a vertical one, undecorated except by the application of a perfectly judged quantity of pure color. This architecture was intended neither to excite nor to distract. On the contrary, "in this new environment a man can be seen. Everything has been thought out. Against these big calm areas the human face assumes its rightful status. A nose, an eye, a foot, a hand or a jacket button becomes a precise reality." As with this imagined architecture, so with the paintings: an aesthetic of concern reinvented the notion of human dignity. This is something that every generation has to do for itself; but there are times when a shared concern has seemed to sweep across the civilized world, and the period which we have examined here was one of them.

54. Ludwig Mies van der Rohe
    and Philip Johnson
Seagram Administration Building,
    New York, 1954–58

SUGGESTED READINGS

General

Giedion, Sigfried. *Space, Time and Architecture*. Rev. and enl. 5th edition.
Cambridge, Mass., Harvard University Press, 1973.

Bauhaus

Bayer, Herbert, Gropius, Ise, and Gropius, Walter. *Bauhaus, 1919–1928*.
Introduction by Alfred H. Barr, Jr.
New York, The Museum of Modern Art, 1938.

Gropius, Walter. *The New Architecture and the Bauhaus*.
Shand, P. Morton, tr. First publ. 1936.
Boston, Charles T. Branford, 1955.

Itten, Johannes. *Design and Form: The Basic Course at the Bauhaus*.
New York, Reinhold, 1964.

Naylor, Gillian. *The Bauhaus*.
London, Studio Vista; New York, E. P. Dutton, 1968.

Neumann, Eckhard, ed. *Bauhaus and Bauhaus People*.
New York, Nostrand Reinhold, 1970.

Wingler, Hans M. *The Bauhaus: Weimar, Dessau, Berlin, Chicago*.
Cambridge, Mass., MIT Press, 1969.

De Stijl

Jaffé, Hans L. C. *De Stijl, 1917–1931*.
New York, Abrams, 1971.

The Russians

Gray, Camilla. *The Russian Experiment in Art: 1863–1922*.
London, Thames and Hudson, 1971.

Shvidkovsky, O. A., ed. *Building in the USSR, 1917–1932*.
New York, Praeger, 1971.

Marcel Breuer

Jones, Cranston. *Marcel Breuer: Buildings and Projects, 1921–1961*.
New York, Praeger, 1962.

Naum Gabo

Gabo, Naum. *Naum Gabo: Constructions, Sculpture, Paintings, Drawings, Engravings*. Introductory essays by Herbert Read and Leslie Martin.
Cambridge, Mass., Harvard University Press, 1957.

Walter Gropius

Giedion, Sigfried. *Walter Gropius: Work and Teamwork*.
New York, Reinhold, 1954.

Gropius, Walter. *Apollo in the Democracy: The Cultural Obligation of the Architect*.
New York, McGraw-Hill, 1968.

Paul Klee

Grohmann, Will. *Paul Klee*. First publ. 1954.
New York, Abrams, 1966.

Haftmann, Werner. *The Inward Vision: Watercolors, Drawings, Writings*.
New York, Abrams, 1958.

Klee, Felix. *Paul Klee: His Life and Work in Documents. Selected Posthumous Writings and Unpublished Letters*.
New York, Braziller, 1962.

Klee, Paul. *The Diaries of Paul Klee, 1898–1918*. Felix Klee, ed.
Berkeley, University of California Press, 1964.

Muller, Joseph-Emile. *Klee: Figures and Masks*.
New York, Tudor, 1961.

Le Corbusier

Besset, Maurice. *Who Was Le Corbusier?*
Geneva, Skira (distributed by The World Publishing Company), 1968.

Boesiger, Willy, and Girsberger, Hans, eds. *Le Corbusier, 1910–1965*.
New York, Praeger, 1967.

Choay, Françoise. *Le Corbusier*. (Masters of World Architecture ser.)
New York, Braziller, 1960.

El Lissitzky

Lissitzky, El, and Arp, Jean. *The Isms of Art.*
New York, Arno, 1968.

Lissitzky-Küppers, Sophie, ed. *El Lissitzky: Life, Letters, Texts.*
Introduction by Herbert Read.
Greenwich, Conn., New York Graphic Society, 1968.

Ludwig Mies van der Rohe

Blaser, Werner. *Mies van der Rohe: The Art of Structure.*
New York, Praeger, 1965.

Drexler, Arthur. *Ludwig Mies van der Rohe.* (Masters of World Architecture ser.)
New York, Braziller, 1960.

Kasimir Malevich

Andersen, Troels. *Malevich.* (Catalogue raisonné)
Amsterdam, Stedelijk Museum, 1970.

Malevich, Kasimir. *Essays on Art: 1915–1933.* Andersen, Troels, ed.
(Documents of Modern Art ser.)
New York, Wittenborn, 1971.

László Moholy-Nagy

Kostelanetz, Richard, ed. *Moholy-Nagy.*
(Documentary Monographs in Modern Art).
New York, Praeger, 1970.

Moholy-Nagy, László. *Vision in Motion.*
Chicago, Theobald, 1947.

Moholy-Nagy, László. *Painting, Photography, Film.*
Cambridge, Mass., MIT Press, 1969.

Piet Mondrian

Busignani, Alberto. *Mondrian.*
New York, Grosset and Dunlap, 1968.

Hunter, Sam. *Mondrian Portfolio.*
New York, Abrams, 1971.

Jaffé, Hans L. C. *Piet Mondrian.*
New York, Abrams, 1970.

Welsh, Robert P., and Joosten, J. M., eds.
Two Mondrian Sketchbooks, 1912–1914.
Amsterdam, Meulenhoff, 1969.

Frank Lloyd Wright

James, Cary. *The Imperial Hotel: Frank Lloyd Wright and the Architecture of Unity.*
Rutland, Vermont, Charles E. Tuttle, 1968.

Drexler, Arthur. *The Drawings of Frank Lloyd Wright.*
New York, Horizon, 1962.

Farr, Finis. *Frank Lloyd Wright: A Biography.*
New York, Scribners, 1961.

Scully, Vincent, Jr. *Frank Lloyd Wright.* (Masters of World Architecture ser.)
New York, Braziller, 1960.

Wright, Frank Lloyd. *Frank Lloyd Wright: Writings and Buildings.*
Kaufman, Edgar, Jr., and Raeburn, Ben, eds.
New York, Horizon, 1960.

Wright, Frank Lloyd. *Buildings, Plans and Designs.*
New York, Horizon, 1963.

LIST OF ILLUSTRATIONS

Dimensions: height precedes width; another dimension, depth, is given for sculptures and constructions where relevant. Foreign titles are in English, except in cases where the title does not translate or is better known in its original form. Asterisked titles indicate works reproduced in color.

Anonymous

Warehouses near New Quay, Liverpool, Lancashire; 19th century (fig. 5)

Bayer, Herbert
(b. 1900)

Kandinsky zum 60. Geburtstag (Kandinsky's 60th Birthday), 1926 (fig. 37)
Offset lithograph, 19 x 25 inches
The Museum of Modern Art, New York
Gift of Mr. and Mrs. Alfred H. Barr, Jr.

Beggarstaff Brothers
(William Nicholson, 1872–1949)
(James Pryde, 1866–1941)

Rowntree's Elect Cocoa, 1895 (fig. 2)
Lithograph, 38 x 28⅝ inches
The Museum of Modern Art, New York
Gift of the Estate of C. M. Price

Breuer, Marcel
(b. 1902)

Whitney Museum of American Art, New York, 1963–66 (fig. 35)

Chagall, Marc
(b. 1887)

The Wedding, 1910 (fig. 1)
Oil on canvas, 39 x 75 inches
Private collection

Forward! 1917 (pl. I)
Gouache, 15 x 9¼ inches (sight)
Art Gallery of Ontario, Toronto
Gift of Sam and Ayala Zacks, 1970

Doesburg, Theo van
(1883–1931)

Composition: The Cow, 1916–17 (fig. 3)
Oil on canvas, 14¾ x 25 inches
The Museum of Modern Art, New York
Purchase

(in collaboration with Cornelis van Eesteren)
Color Construction, 1922
(project for a private house; pl. II)
Gouache and ink, 22½ x 22½ inches
The Museum of Modern Art, New York
Edgar Kaufmann, Jr., Fund

Feininger, Lyonel
(1871–1956)

Cathedral, 1919 (fig. 39)
Woodcut, 5⅜ x 3½ inches
The Museum of Modern Art, New York
Gift of Abby Aldrich Rockefeller

Gabo, Naum
(b. 1890)

Head of a Woman, c. 1917–20 (fig. 19)
Construction in celluloid and metal, 24½ x 19¼ inches
The Museum of Modern Art, New York
Purchase

Column, 1923 (fig. 20)
Plastic, wood and metal, 41 inches high
The Solomon R. Guggenheim Museum, New York

Guimard, Hector
(1867–1942)

Entrance to Métro Station, Paris, c. 1900 (fig. 4)
Cast iron, painted green with amber colored glass lampshades, 15 feet 5 inches x 21 feet
The Museum of Modern Art, New York
Gift of Régie Autonome des Transports Parisiens

Gropius, Walter
(1883–1969)

The Bauhaus, Dessau, 1925–26 (fig. 42)

Kandinsky, Wassily
(1866–1944)

Composition 8, 1923 (fig. 45)
Oil on canvas, 55½ x 79⅛ inches
The Solomon R. Guggenheim Museum, New York

Klee, Paul
(1879–1940)

The Hopeless Ones, 1914 (fig. 46)
Watercolor, 5 x 8½ inches
Marian Willard Johnson, New York

The End of the Last Act of a Drama, 1920 (fig. 47)
Watercolor on transfer drawing, 8⅛ x 11⅜ inches
The Museum of Modern Art, New York
Gift of Dr. and Mrs. Allan Roos

Begrüssung (Greeting), 1922 (fig. 48)
Watercolor, 8¾ x 12¼ inches
Wadsworth Atheneum, Hartford, Conn.
Ella Gallup Sumner and Mary Catlin Sumner Collection

Building the L-Platz, 1923 (pl. X)
Watercolor, gouache, chalk and newsprint on cardboard, 15¾ x 20½ inches
Kunstsammlung Nordrhein-Westfalen, Düsseldorf

Pastorale, 1927 (fig. 49)
Tempera on canvas, mounted on wood, 27¼ x 20⅝ inches
The Museum of Modern Art, New York
Abby Aldrich Rockefeller Fund and exchange

Fire in the Evening, 1929 (pl. XI)
Oil on cardboard, 13⅜ x 13¼ inches
The Museum of Modern Art, New York
Mr. and Mrs. Joachim Jean Aberbach Fund

Larionov, Mikhail
(1881–1964)

Portrait of Vladimir Tatlin in Seaman's Blouse, 1908 (fig. 23)
Oil on canvas, 30¼ x 23¼ inches
Private collection

Le Corbusier (Charles-Edouard Jeanneret)
(1887–1965)

Still Life, 1920 (fig. 52)
Oil on canvas, 31⅞ x 39¼ inches
The Museum of Modern Art, New York
Van Gogh Purchase Fund

Le Corbusier (continued)

(in collaboration with Pierre Jeanneret)
Model of Villa Savoye (1929–31) at Poissy, France
(fig. 8)
Wood, aluminum and plastic, 33⅞ x 31½ x 14½
inches
The Museum of Modern Art, New York

Léger, Fernand
(1881–1955)

The City, 1919 (fig. 51)
Oil on canvas, 6 feet 6¾ inches x 9 feet 9¼ inches
Philadelphia Museum of Art
The A. E. Gallatin Collection

The Mechanic, 1920 (fig. 50)
Oil on canvas, 45½ x 34¾ inches
The National Gallery of Canada, Ottawa

*Three Women (Le Grand Déjeuner), 1921 (pl. XII)
Oil on canvas, 72¼ x 99 inches
The Museum of Modern Art, New York
Mrs. Simon Guggenheim Fund

Lissitzky, El (Eliezer)
(1890–1941)

Plate 10: "The New One," from the portfolio
Victory Over the Sun, 1923 (fig. 21)
Lithograph, 21 x 13¾ inches
The Museum of Modern Art, New York
Purchase

Model of the set for *I Want a Child*
(by Sergei Tretyakov) commissioned by
Meyerhold for production at his theater in
Moscow, 1926–29 (fig. 25)
Photograph courtesy The Arts Council of
Great Britain, London

Malevich, Kasimir
(1878–1935)

Morning in the Village after Snowfall, 1912
(fig. 28)
Oil on canvas, 31½ x 31⅜ inches
The Solomon R. Guggenheim Museum, New York

Head of a Peasant Girl, 1912 (fig. 30)
Oil on canvas, 32 x 38 inches
Stedelijk Museum, Amsterdam

*Woman with Water Pails: Dynamic Arrangement,
1912 (pl. VII)
Oil on canvas, 31⅝ x 31⅝ inches
The Museum of Modern Art, New York

Private of the First Division, 1914 (fig. 29)
Oil on canvas, with collage of postage stamp,
thermometer, etc., 21⅛ x 17⅝ inches
The Museum of Modern Art, New York

Suprematist Composition (Airplane Flying), 1914
(fig. 33)
Oil on canvas, 22⅞ x 19 inches
The Museum of Modern Art, New York
Purchase

*Suprematist Composition, 1916–17(?) (pl. IX)
Oil on canvas, 38½ x 26⅛ inches
The Museum of Modern Art, New York

Suprematist Composition: White on White,
1918(?) (fig. 31)
Oil on canvas, 31¼ x 31¼ inches
The Museum of Modern Art, New York

Suprematist Painting, after 1920 (fig. 32)
Oil on canvas, 33½ x 27½ inches
Stedelijk Museum, Amsterdam

*Suprematist Architectural Drawing (Future Planits
for Leningrad: The Pilot's Planit),* 1924
(fig. 34)
Pencil, 12¼ x 17⅜ inches
The Museum of Modern Art, New York
Purchase

Mies van der Rohe, Ludwig
(1886–1969)

Lounge Chair ("Barcelona" Chair), 1929 (fig. 36)
Chrome-plated steel bars and leather, 29½ inches
high
The Museum of Modern Art, New York
Gift of Knoll Associates, Inc.

Mies van der Rohe, Ludwig,
and Johnson, Philip (b. 1906)

Seagram Administration Building, New York,
1954–58 (fig. 54)

Moholy-Nagy, László
(1895–1946)

Light-Space Modulator, 1923–30 (fig. 43)
Metal, glass and plastic, 59½ x 27½ x 27½ inches
Busch-Reisinger Museum, Harvard University,
Cambridge, Mass.

Nudes on the Grass, 1929 (fig. 44)
Photograph: negative print from positive
transparency
The Museum of Modern Art, New York
Given anonymously

Mondrian, Piet
(1872–1944)

Self-Portrait, c. 1900 (fig. 9)
Oil on canvas, mounted on composition board,
19⅞ x 15½ inches
The Phillips Collection, Washington, D.C.

Red Amaryllis with Blue Background, c. 1907
(fig. 10)
Watercolor, 18⅜ x 13 inches
The Museum of Modern Art, New York
The Sidney and Harriet Janis Collection

*Woods near Oele, 1908 (pl. IV)
Oil on canvas, 51 x 63 inches
Gemeentemuseum, The Hague

Still Life with Ginger Pot II, 1912 (fig. 11)
Oil on canvas, 36 x 47¼ inches
Gemeentemuseum, The Hague

Paris Buildings (rue du Départ), c. 1912–13 (fig. 12)
Pencil, 9¼ x 6 inches
Sidney Janis Gallery Collection, New York

Blue Façade (Composition 9), 1913–14 (fig. 13)
Oil on canvas, 37½ x 26⅝ inches
The Museum of Modern Art, New York
Gift of Mr. and Mrs. Armand P. Bartos

Pier and Ocean, 1914 (fig. 14)
Charcoal and watercolor, 34⅝ x 44 inches
The Museum of Modern Art, New York
Mrs. Simon Guggenheim Fund

Composition with Color Planes, V, 1917 (fig. 15)
Oil on canvas, 19⅜ x 24⅛ inches
The Museum of Modern Art, New York
The Sidney and Harriet Janis Collection

***Composition C,* 1920 (pl. V)
Oil on canvas, 23¾ x 24 inches
The Museum of Modern Art, New York
Acquired through the Lillie P. Bliss Bequest

***Composition,* 1925 (pl. VI)
Oil on canvas, 15⅞ x 12⅝ inches
The Museum of Modern Art, New York
Gift of Philip Johnson

Painting I, 1926 (fig. 16)
Oil on canvas, diagonal 44¾ x 44 inches
The Museum of Modern Art, New York
Katherine S. Dreier Bequest

Nicholson, Ben
(b. 1894)

White Relief, 1936 (fig. 17)
Oil on carved board, 42 x 53½ inches
Dallas Museum of Fine Arts
Foundation for the Arts Collection

Ozenfant, Amédée
(1886–1966)

Fugue, 1925 (fig. 53)
Pencil, 18 x 22 inches
The Museum of Modern Art, New York
Gift of the artist

Poelzig, Hans
(1869–1936)

End wall of the Chemical Factory in Luban, near Posen, Germany, 1911–12 (fig. 6)
Photograph courtesy Universitätsbibliothek der Technischen Universität, Berlin

Popova, Liubov
(1889–1924)

Architectonic Painting, 1917 (fig. 27)
Oil on canvas, 31½ x 38⅝ inches
The Museum of Modern Art, New York
Philip Johnson Fund

Model of the set for *The Magnanimous Cuckold* (by Fernand Crommelynck) produced by Meyerhold at the Nezlobin Theater, Moscow, 1922 (fig. 26)
Photograph courtesy The Arts Council of Great Britain, London

Puni, Ivan
(1894–1956)

***Bath,* 1915 (pl. VIII)
Oil on canvas, 28¾ x 36¼ inches
Private collection

Rietveld, Gerrit Thomas
(1888–1964)

***Red and Blue Armchair,* 1918 (pl. III)
Painted wood, 34½ inches high
The Museum of Modern Art, New York
Gift of Philip Johnson

Schröder House, Utrecht, Holland, 1924 (fig. 18)
The Museum of Modern Art, New York
Architectural Department Photo Archive

Schlemmer, Oskar
(1888–1943)

Study for "The Triadic Ballet," 1922 (fig. 40)
Gouache, ink and collage of photographs, 22⅝ x 14⅝ inches
The Museum of Modern Art, New York
Gift of Mr. and Mrs. Douglas Auchincloss

Bauhaus Stairway, 1932 (fig. 41)
Oil on canvas, 63⅞ x 45 inches
The Museum of Modern Art, New York
Gift of Philip Johnson

Tatlin, Vladimir
(1885–1953)

Project for the Monument to the Third International, 1919–20 (fig. 22) (reconstruction)
Photograph courtesy The Arts Council of Great Britain, London

Tschichold, Jan
(1902–1974)

Buster Keaton in: "Der General," (fig. 38)
Poster, 47¾ x 32½ inches
The Museum of Modern Art, New York
Gift of the artist

Vesnin Brothers
(Victor Vesnin, 1882–1950)
(Alexander Vesnin, b. 1883)

Project for the Leningrad "Pravda" Building, 1923–24 (fig. 24) (reconstruction)
Photograph courtesy The Arts Council of Great Britain, London

Wright, Frank Lloyd
(1869–1959)

Frederick C. Robie House, Chicago, Illinois, 1909 (fig. 7)

PHOTOGRAPH CREDITS

Oliver Baker, New York, 12; E. Irving Blomstrann, New Britain, Conn., 48; Bill Engdahl, Hedrich-Blessing, Chicago, 7; Kate Keller, New York, 21, III, V, VI, IX, XI; Eric de Maré, London, 5; James Mathews, New York, 10, 15, 37, 38; Rolf Petersen, New York, 2; Stan Ries, New York, 4, 36, II; Ezra Stoller, Mamaroneck, N.Y., 35; Sunami, 3, 13, 14, 16, 19, 22, 27, 29, 31, 33, 34, 39, 40, 41, 47, 49, 52, 53; Rodney Todd-White, London, 22; Ron Vickers, Toronto, I; John Webb, London, 24, 25, 26.